THE BRITISH MUSEUM

Illustrated Encyclopaedia of

ANCIENT GREECE

Sean Sheehan

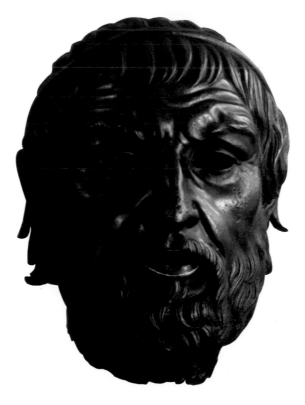

THE BRITISH MUSEUM PRESS

Sean Sheehan has asserted his right to be identified as the author of this Work

First published in 2002 by The British Museum Press
A division of The British Museum Company Ltd
46 Bloomsbury Street, London WC1B 3QQ

A catalogue record for this book is available from the British Library

ISBN 0 7141 2179 7

Designed and typeset in Novarese Book by Bender Richardson White, P O Box 266, Uxbridge UB9 5NX
Design: Ben White and Malcolm Smythe
Editorial: Lionel Bender and Mike March
Production: Kim Richardson

Printed and bound in Hong Kong, by C&C Offset

Author's Acknowledgements

The author would like to thank all those who have helped by reading the text and making valuable improvements, especially Richard Woff and John Hazel. A special thank you to Carolyn Jones at the British Museum Press whose ability to blend patience with professionalism has made this book possible.

Author's Dedication

This encyclopaedia is dedicated to Joseph and Danny who one day - I hope - will also wonder what was so special about the ancient Greeks.

Illustration acknowledgements

Pictures are © The British Museum, photos taken by the British Museum Photographic and Imaging Department, with the exception of those listed below.

Map artwork by Stefan Chabluk.

Trail icons and drawings on pp 18, 34, 82, 86 by Stefan Chabluk.

P. 8 left: Pencil drawing by C.R. Cockerell.
p. 9 top: Venus Weeping over Adonis, c.1625 (oil on canvas) by Nicolas Poussin (1594-1665), Musée des Beaux Arts, Caen, France/Giraudon/The Bridgeman Art Library.
p. 11 top Lesley and Roy Adkins Picture Library.
p. 15 bottom: The Metamorphosis of Daphne (tempera on panel), by the Master of the Judgement of Paris (fl. 1450), The Barber Institute of Fine Arts, University of Brimingham/Bridgeman Art Library.
p. 16: Lesley and Roy Adkins Picture Library.
p. 17: Drawing by Sarah Warburton.
p. 19 left: Bacchus and Ariadne (oil on canvas) by Titian (d.1576), The National Gallery, London.
p. 19 right: Chloe Productions.
p. 20: Raphael, The School at Athens, SCALA SPA.
p. 22 left: Turkish Tourist Board.
p. 25: Joint Library of the Hellenic and Roman Societies. Slide Collection.
p. 30 left: Sarah Warburton.
p. 32 right: Psyche and Charon by John Roddam Spencer Stanhope (1829–1908), Roy Miles Fine Paintings /Bridgeman Art Library.
p. 33 right: Circe and her Lovers in a Landscape by Dosso Dossi, Samuel H. Kress Collection, photograph © 2000 Board of Trustees, National Gallery of Art, Washington.
p. 35 bottom: Peter Clayton.
p. 36 top: Drawing by Catherine Wood.
p. 36 bottom: Lesley and Roy Adkins Picture Library.
p. 40 bottom: Sally-Ann Ashton.
p. 41 right: The Louvre, photo © RMN / Hervé Lewandowski.
p. 43 left: Pieter Breughel, The Fall of Icarus, Musées Royaux des Beaux-Arts de Belgique, Bruxelles / SCALA SPA.

p. 43 right: Sally-Ann Ashton.
p. 48 top: Chloe Productions.
p. 50 bottom: photo Graham Harrison, © The British Museum.
p. 53 bottom: Joint Library of the Hellenic and Roman Societies. Slide Collection.
p. 56 left: Lesley and Roy Adkins Picture Library.
p. 60: Lesley and Roy Adkins Picture Library.
p. 76: Peter Clayton.
p. 81 left: Peter Clayton.
p. 81 right: Peter Clayton.
p. 84 left: The University of Manchester.
p. 89: Medusa, painted on a leather jousting shield by Michelangelo Merisi da Caravaggio (1571–1610), Galleria degli Uffizi/Bridgeman Art Library.
p. 92 bottom: Peter Clayton.
p. 95: J. Lesley Fitton.
p. 102: Oedipus and the Sphinx, 1808 (oil on canvas) by Jean Auguste Dominique Ingres (1780-1867), Louvre, Paris, France/Giraudon/Bridgeman Art Library.
p. 103: Peter Clayton.
p. 105 bottom: Action Plus/photo Glyn Kirk.
p. 106 bottom: Joint Library of the Hellenic and Roman Societies. Slide Collection.
p. 110: The Triumph of Pan (oil on canvas) by Nicolas Poussin (1594-1665), The National Gallery, London.
p. 112-3: Peter Clayton.
p. 116: Penelope with the Suitors (fresco, detached and mounted on canvas) by Pintoricchio (d. 1513), The National Gallery, London.
p. 119 left: Sarah Warburton.
p. 122 top: Kate Morton.
p. 123 right: Prometheus, 1868, oil on canvas, by Gustave Moreau (1826–98), Musée Gustave Moreau, Paris, France/Bridgeman Art Library.
p. 133 left: Chloe Productions.
p. 135 top: Sally-Ann Ashton.
p. 137 top: Peter Clayton.
p. 140 bottom: Lesley and Roy Adkins Picture Library.
p. 141: Lesley and Roy Adkins Picture Library.
p. 152: Lesley and Roy Adkins Picture Library.

Contents

How to use this book
The encyclopaedia has entries in A–Z order. You can look up information on ancient Greek people, places, things and ideas by name. For example: **Achilles**, **Sparta**, **Clothes**, **Fate**.

Inside the entries you will see words printed in **bold type**. That means the word has an encyclopaedia entry of its own that you can look up.

If you are not sure where to start in the A–Z entries, you can try following a Greek trail – look on pages 6 to 7 for a list of Trails on different topics.

If you can't find something in the main part of the book, try looking in the index on page 158.

The spelling of Greek names
The ancient Greeks used an alphabet that looks rather different from ours. We have to change Greek names into our alphabet so that we can read them. In the past the Greek names have not always been changed in a very accurate way.

People who study ancient Greece today are trying more and more to use spellings that are close to the original Greek, but this makes some of the words look rather strange to most of us. Sometimes the differences are very small – for example, Dionysus would change to Dionysos and Electra would be Elektra. Sometimes the differences are greater. You might not realize straight away that Croesus is the same person as Kroisos!

In this encyclopaedia we have used Greek names in their more well-known spellings, so that they are easier to read and recognize. In the A-Z entries you'll find **Dionysus** and **Electra** and **Croesus**. But if there is a more historically correct spelling we have put it in brackets afterwards: for example, **Achilles (Akhilleus)**.

The extent of the ancient Greek world.

Trails

Follow a Greek trail!
To help you find your way around the Encyclopaedia, there are a number of 'Trails' to follow.

This is how to follow a trail:
Look at the headings on these two pages and decide which topic you are most interested in. Let's say you want to follow the Trail that will lead you to information on Gods and Goddesses. Under 'Gods and Goddesses' you'll find a list of words or terms. For each of these there's an entry in the Encyclopaedia with information on your chosen topic. The entries are in alphabetical order throughout the book, so it should be easy to find the ones you want. Look up the items in the list – each will tell you something different about Gods and Goddesses.

Every trail is identified by its own little icon. This icon is the one that will help you spot the Gods and Goddesses entries.

If you prefer, you can just browse through the Encyclopaedia. Whenever you see this icon under a title, you know that the entry below contains information on Gods and Goddesses.

All the trails can be followed in the same way.

You can also use the index on page 158 to find what you are looking for.

Happy hunting!

Art & Architecture

Architecture
Athens
Elgin Marbles
Erechtheum
Knossos
Minoan civilization
Music
Painting
Parthenon
Phidias
Pottery
Sculpture
Temples

Everyday Life

Babyhood
Childhood
Climate
Clothes
Coins
Cooking
Education
Farming
Festivals
Food
Funerals
Furniture
Gymnasium
Hairstyles
Houses
Hunting
Marriage
Medicine
Money
Olives
Slaves
Transport
Washing and
    cosmetics
Water
Wine
Writing and reading

Ideas

Archimedes
Aristotle
Competition
Democracy
Fate
Friendship
Hubris
Law
Mathematics
Nemesis
Oligarchy
Philosophy
Plato
Revenge
Shame
Socrates
Tyranny

Gods & Goddesses

Aphrodite
Apollo
Artemis
Athena
Demeter and
    Persephone
Dionysus
Eros
Hades
Hephaestus
Hera
Hermes
Nemesis
Nike
Pan
Poseidon
Zeus

Legacy of Greece

Architecture
Athletics
Classical Age
Democracy
Drama
Hellenistic Age
History of Greece
Language
Myth
Olympic Games
Philosophy
Theatres

Myths

Adonis
Andromeda
Ariadne
Atlantis
Atlas
Centaurs
Creation Myth
Cyclopes
Daedalus & Icarus
Electra
Eurydice
Harpies
Heracles
Jason and the
    Argonauts
Medusa
Myth
Narcissus
Odysseus
Oedipus
Pandora
Pegasus
Perseus
Satyrs
Sirens
Theseus
Trojan War

Theatre & Drama

Aeschylus
Aristophanes
Chorus
Dionysia
Drama
Euripides
Festivals
Sophocles
Theatres

Greece & Her Neighbours

Africa
Asia Minor
Athens
Barbarians
City-state
Colonies
Crete
Egypt
Greece
Greeks
History of Greece
Ionia
Italy
Lydia
Macedon
Mediterranean
Minoan civilization
Mycenae
Persia
Phoenicia
Rome
Scythians
Sicily
Sparta
Thebes
Thessaly
Thrace

Religion

Dionysia
Eleusinian Mysteries
Festivals
Hades
Magic
Olympus
Oracles
Panathenaea
Priests and
    Priestesses
Prophecies
Religion
Sacrifices
Temples
Thesmophoria

Warfare

Alexander the Great
Armour and arms
Cavalry
Marathon
Mercenaries
Navy
Peloponnesian War
Pericles
Persian Wars
Plataea
Sieges
Thermopylae
Trojan War
War
Warfare
Xerxes

Sport & Leisure

Athletics
Boxing
Chariot Races
Discus
Drama
Gymnasium
Olympic Games
Stadium
Symposium
Toys and games
Wrestling

Troy

Achilles
Agamemnon
Ajax
Bronze Age
Cassandra
Hector
Helen
Homer
Iliad
Odysseus
Trojan War
Wooden Horse

Writers

Aeschylus
Aesop
Aristophanes
Aristotle
Euripides
Herodotus
Hesiod
Homer
Plato
Sappho
Sophocles
Thucydides
Xenophon

A

Achilles (Akhilleus)

Achilles was a great hero in the **Trojan War**. His mother was a goddess called Thetis but his father Peleus was human. The only part of Achilles that could be injured was his heel. This was because his mother bathed him in the river Styx to make him invulnerable and she held him by the heel when she dipped him in the magical water. When Achilles grew up, his mother warned him that going to **Troy** meant a short but glorious life, whereas a long but quiet life would be his **fate** if he stayed at home. Achilles chose to fight at Troy.

Achilles withdrew from fighting at Troy after a quarrel with **Agamemnon**. When Achilles did return to the battle-field, he killed the Trojan prince **Hector** in a fit of anger and only released the dead body when Hector's father begged him to do so. In the **Iliad**, by the poet **Homer**, Achilles emerges as a heroic warrior who can act savagely at times. He values his honour above his life, but he is also very human and aware of his own mortality.

Achilles fights the Trojan warrior Memnon.

Acropolis

Acropolis is a Greek word meaning 'top of the city'. Many Greek settlements were based around a hilltop or other high point that could readily be defended against attack. Usually, an acropolis would also be a sacred site, where temples and monuments were built. The most famous acropolis of all is at **Athens**.

*A drawing of the **Acropolis** in **Athens**, made in the early 1800s. The building at the top on the right is the **Parthenon**.*

When the Persians invaded Greece (see **Persian Wars**) they occupied Athens and destroyed the buildings on the Acropolis. After the defeat of the Persians, the people of Athens set about rebuilding the temples. They wanted to celebrate and thank the gods for their victory. The **Parthenon** and the **Erechtheum**, built in the 5th century BC, are some of the noted buildings on the Acropolis that have survived.

Adonis

Adonis was a beautiful young man. When he was a child, the goddess **Aphrodite** was so moved by his beauty that she secretly entrusted him to another

'My dramas are but slices cut off the great banquet of Homer's poems.'
Aeschylus

The story of the Oresteia by **Aeschylus** was well known to the Greeks. This vase illustrates one part of it, the pursuit of Orestes (in the centre) by the Furies.

goddess, Persephone. But then Persephone herself wanted to keep him. The jealousy between the two goddesses was settled by Adonis spending part of the year with each of them.

While still a young man, Adonis was gored to death by a wild boar. When Aphrodite cried, a rose came from each of her tears and the same number of anemone flowers came from the drops of blood that Adonis shed.

Aeschylus (Aiskylos)

Aeschylus (525–456 BC) was the earliest of the three great playwrights from 5th-century **Athens**. The others were **Sophocles** and **Euripides**. Aeschylus was thirty-five when he fought against the Persians at **Marathon**. Six years later he won first prize at the Festival of Dionysus (**Dionysia**) for a group of three tragic plays that have not survived.

Today, Aeschylus is best known for another group of plays, the Oresteia, which have survived. They tell the story of how **Agamemnon**, after returning from **Troy**, is murdered by his wife, Clytemnestra, and her lover. Agamemnon's son, **Orestes**, seeks revenge and kills Clytemnestra with the support of his sister, **Electra**. Orestes is then pursued by the Furies, supernatural beings who demand their own revenge for this shedding of family blood. In the last of the three plays, Orestes is put on trial in an Athenian court. With the help of **Athena**, the court finds a peaceful and lawful solution. Orestes is declared innocent and the Furies are invited to stay in Athens.

Aesop

Aesop was the author of a famous collection of fables that often feature animals as characters. Next to nothing is known about Aesop, although he probably lived between around 620 and 560 BC. The historian **Herodotus** says he was a slave on the island of Samos.

One of Aesop's most famous tales tells how a slow but steady tortoise wins a race against a much faster hare. The hare thinks he can afford to stop for a mid-race nap, but when he wakes he cannot catch up with the tortoise, who wins the race. The story is typical of Aesop's fables. It teaches a lesson that the weak or disadvantaged can always make the best of their situation, and sometimes come out on top. Such a moral would certainly have appealed to slaves, so perhaps Herodotus was right about Aesop being a slave.

Africa

The Greeks came into contact with Africa through their trade with **Egypt**. This contact also made the Greeks aware of

*This Greek bronze portrait of a North African is evidence of the ancient Greeks' contact with North **Africa**.*

Egypt's neighbour to the south, Nubia (part of modern Sudan). The historian **Herodotus** speaks of the people of Aithiopia (Ethiopia) as 'the tallest and most attractive people in the world'. The awareness of black people is reflected in Greek art and also finds its way into Greek myth.

Agamemnon

In myth, Agamemnon was a king of **Mycenae** who was married to Clytemnestra. Their children were **Orestes**, **Electra**, and **Iphigenia**.

Agamemnon's brother, Menelaus, was the king of **Sparta**. Menelaus' wife, **Helen**, left her husband and sailed off to **Troy** with a prince called **Paris**. Agamemnon decided to seek **revenge** for his brother and led the Greek expedition to Troy that resulted in the **Trojan War**. Agamemnon was the commander-in-chief at Troy but he had a quarrel with **Achilles** over one of the female war captives. Achilles then refused to fight, and this story becomes a major part of the **Iliad**'s plot.

Agamemnon returned home at the end of the war with the Trojan princess **Cassandra** as his prisoner. When they arrived back in Mycenae, both of them were murdered by Clytemnestra and her lover, Aegisthus. This story, and its sequel when Orestes and Electra seek revenge for the murder of their father, became a favourite with playwrights such as **Aeschylus**.

The story of Agamemnon's other daughter, Iphigenia, was also the subject of plays. Agamemnon was told he needed to sacrifice Iphigenia because he had angered the goddess **Artemis** by killing a stag and boasting that he was a better hunter than the goddess.

*The remains of the **agora** at **Athens**. People would gather in the agora to discuss business and conduct commerce. It was common for an agora to have various statues and shrines, and a **water** fountain.*

Agora

Agora in Greek means 'market place'. In an ancient Greek city, the agora was an open space, usually in a central area, where roads met. It was a place where people could gather and talk as well as a commercial centre where traders set up their stalls.

The warm, sunny climate and the agricultural way of life in ancient Greece made it natural to conduct much business outdoors, so the agora was a vital part of any **city-state**. Sometimes, public buildings adjoined the agora, such as the Painted Colonnade in **Athens** where paintings were displayed.

Ajax (Aias)

The Greek warrior Aias is better known by the Latin version of his name, Ajax. He was second only to **Achilles** in strength and fame as a fighter on the Greek side in the **Trojan War.** Ajax was the son of a king who ruled the island of Salamis (see map, page 62).

He brought twelve ships to **Troy**, and the **Iliad** tells the story of a duel between Ajax and the Trojan leader **Hector**, which neither of them could win. After the death of Achilles, according to one legend, his weapons were presented to **Odysseus** instead of to Ajax. This caused Ajax to become so angry that he went mad and killed himself (see **shame**). That is why in the **Odyssey**, when Odysseus journeys to **Hades** (the Underworld), Ajax refuses to speak to him.

There was another Greek hero, also called Ajax, who fought bravely at Troy. He was known as the Lesser Ajax. The Lesser Ajax also had a reputation for arrogance, and the gods destroyed him because of this.

*This vase shows two warriors (probably **Ajax** and **Achilles**) playing a game while the goddess **Athena** stands between them.*

Alexander the Great

Alexander (356–323 BC) was twenty when he inherited the kingdom of **Macedon** on the death of his father, Philip. Over the next thirteen years he built up the largest empire the world had ever seen, stretching eastwards from Greece as far as Pakistan.

At the age of nine he is said to have tamed a wild horse, Bucephalus, which he kept and rode into the many battles that made Alexander a legend in his own lifetime. His teacher was the philosopher **Aristotle**, and Alexander is said to have sent him back specimens of unusual plants that he discovered on his adventures into strange new lands.

Determined to fulfil his father's ambition to conquer

*A marble head of **Alexander** made in the 2nd-1st century BC.*

*On this coin **Alexander** wears the ram's horn of Amun, an Egyptian god, to indicate his own divinity.*

the mighty empire of **Persia**, Alexander and his army of over 43,000 men and 5,500 horses set off to invade Greece's old enemy. The core of his army was an infantry phalanx: a close formation of 15,000 soldiers that fought with 6-metre (20 foot) pikes. After defeating the Persians at the Battle of Issus in 333 BC, Alexander moved south into what is now

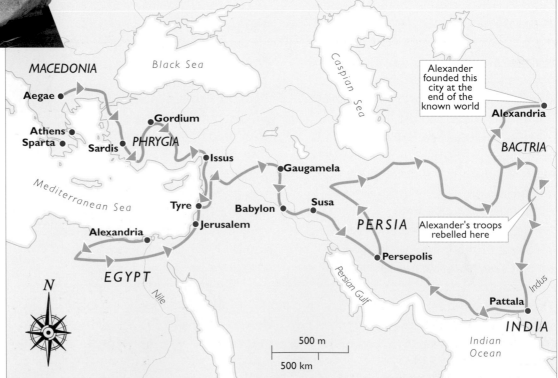

*The map shows the enormous distances that **Alexander** and his army travelled.*

Lebanon, before going on to conquer Egypt and establish a city at the mouth of the Nile, called Alexandria, which still bears his name.

Alexander again defeated the Persians in what is today Iraq. He marched into Babylon and travelled east to the River Indus in modern-day Pakistan. Facing war elephants for the first time, he defeated an opposing force and was ready to continue further east to the River Ganges when his own army mutinied and refused to go on. On the journey back he fell ill in Babylon and died. The great king, who claimed an **oracle** had declared him a living god, was only thirty-three. He was said to have been planning to extend his empire into Arab lands, but after his death his vast empire was divided up between his generals.

The influence of Greek culture remained and made itself felt throughout the Persian empire and in the Indian subcontinent. Alexander himself was a complex character: ruthless and cruel but intelligent, imaginative and very courageous.

Amazons

In **myth** the Amazons were a foreign race of female warriors who lived on the far side of the Black Sea. They hunted and fought on horseback with javelins and excelled with the bow and arrow. They lived in an all-female society, rejecting marriage and having little use for men. To the Greeks they were deadly enemies who had to be defeated.

Achilles killed the Amazon queen, Penthesilea, when her army came to the help of **Troy**. As one of his labours, **Heracles** had to fight the Amazons. **Theseus** also fought against them, as did Bellerophon with the help of **Pegasus**, and a legend claimed that **Alexander the Great** met with an Amazon queen on his travels in the east. Greeks defeating

*Penthesilea, the **Amazon** queen, is about to be killed by **Achilles**. According to legend, Achilles shed tears for the warrior queen after her death.*

Amazons in battle was a favourite subject in Greek art, and the idea of independent, female warriors both fascinated and frightened the Greeks.

***Amazons** were often shown in Greek art like this, fighting on horseback and using the spear, axe and bow as their weapons.*

Anaximander

Anaximander was a philosopher and early scientist from **Miletus** who lived in the 6th century BC. He was one of the group known as **Pre-Socratics**. In about 546 BC he wrote the first Greek book that was not in poetry. It included the first Greek map of the world, showing the Earth hanging unsupported in space. He was a pupil of **Thales** and, like him, believed that the whole of matter was made from one original source. He is said to have thought that human beings first came from the sea as fish that could walk. The Greeks' first sundial is also said to have been built by Anaximander.

Andromeda

In Greek myth Andromeda was the daughter of a king, Cepheus, and his queen Cassiopeia. The queen boasted that she was more beautiful than the Nereids, who were sea goddesses. As a punishment the land was flooded and a sea-monster let loose. Cepheus was told the only way to lift the curse was to sacrifice Andromeda to the sea-monster. She was tied up and left to her fate.

At the time, **Perseus** was returning home after killing the Gorgon **Medusa**, and when he saw the captive Andromeda he pitied her. Perseus killed the sea-monster and freed Andromeda, but they were pursued by her uncle who was betrothed to her. They escaped when Perseus showed Medusa's head to their pursuers, turning them to stone. Perseus and Andromeda journeyed on to his home city of Argos, lived happily there and had many children.

Aphrodite

Aphrodite was the goddess of love and fertility, an important figure to the Greeks. Aphrodite was a powerful goddess. She was worshipped throughout the Greek world and is often shown in Greek art. The Romans called her Venus.

Among the gods, Aphrodite had both friends and enemies. Ares the god of war was one of her lovers, but she came into conflict with Persephone over the custody of **Adonis**. She competed with two other

*A Greek mirror case shows **Aphrodite** and **Pan** playing a game of knucklebones (see **toys and games**). The small winged figure is her son **Eros**. A goose appears beside her. These birds were often associated with Aphrodite.*

*This vase-painting shows **Andromeda** (in the centre) being led to her place of sacrifice. The men on the right are preparing the posts where Andromeda will be tied.*

goddesses, **Hera** and **Athena**, over who was the most beautiful, and **Paris** awarded her the prize after she promised him the hand of the beautiful **Helen**. In this way Aphrodite was responsible for the war at **Troy**, because it was Paris who took Helen to Troy and so caused the Greeks to unite and try to win her back.

Apollo

The god Apollo was the son of **Zeus** and a Titaness, Leto. He had a twin sister, **Artemis**. Apollo is usually portrayed as a beautiful young man and was associated with the dolphin and the bay laurel tree. However, he was capable of terrible disdain for humankind. The Greeks revered him with a deep respect that bordered on fear.

Apollo represented the value of order. He was associated with music and poetry of a calm, measured kind, as opposed to the wilder rhythms of drum and pipes that accompanied **Dionysus**. Two sayings connected with Apollo, 'Know thyself' and 'Nothing in excess', celebrate self-knowledge and moderation. Apollo was also the god of prophecy, and at one of the most important shrines in Greece, at **Delphi**, worshippers came to hear what the god might say about the future.

Apollo was a god of healing, but the Greeks also saw him as the god who brings the sickness that needs healing. The story of the **Iliad** begins with the Greeks being struck down by a plague, caused by arrows fired by Apollo from his bow. Only a show of the utmost respect for the god could bring about a change of heart on his part.

Apollo was also a warrior, who sided with **Troy** against the Greeks even after the Trojan princess **Cassandra** rejected his love.

Above: **Apollo** is often shown as the perfect type of young, male beauty. This is a marble statue of Apollo made in the **Hellenistic Age**.

Left: This painting from the 15th century AD depicts the myth of the **nymph** Daphne. She was pursued by **Apollo**. She prayed to a river god for help and was turned into a laurel tree.

Archaeology

Archaeology is the study of the past through the real objects that survive. Archaeology has provided a wealth of knowledge about ancient Greece as well as the means for preserving many ancient objects. Materials such as **pottery** and stone resist natural decay, so everyday objects like vases and perfume pots, as well as works of art in painted pottery and monumental stone statues, sculptures and even whole temples, have been preserved. Mirrors, musical instruments and other objects made of bronze or other metals have also been found. Materials that quickly decay in the ground, like wood and cloth, are rarely found, so everyday items such as clothes and ordinary buildings like homes have

rarely survived. Archaeologists continue to excavate, date and map large and small sites, under the ground and under the sea, using the latest technology in their fieldwork.

The motives of archaeologists have changed a lot from the early 19th century, when looking for Greek remains first became an organized and serious business. Then it was mostly wealthy men who were keen to find Greek works of art. They would ship them home and often sell to a museum what they had taken. The most spectacular achievements of early archaeology were the discovery of **Troy** and the excavation of **Mycenae** by the amateur archaeologist Heinrich Schliemann in the 1870s. When Schliemann discovered a funeral mask made from a sheet of beaten gold, he

Archaeologists are still excavating the site of ancient Sparta.

thought he was gazing at the face of the great **Agamemnon** himself. The scale of his excavations encouraged other large-scale archaeological expeditions to places such as **Athens** and **Delphi**. In 1900 Arthur Evans made a further great discovery at **Knossos**.

Archimedes
(Arkhimedes)

The famous mathematician and inventor Archimedes lived around 287–211 BC. He came from Syracuse, a Greek colony on the island of **Sicily**. When King Hieron of Syracuse asked him to establish whether other metals had been added to a gold crown, Archimedes discovered an answer while taking a bath. He realized that the amount of water displaced by his sitting in the bath was determined by his size. If he were twice as big then twice as much water would be displaced. This principle could be applied to the crown. If the crown were pure gold it would have to weigh the same as a piece of gold that displaced the same amount of water.

Celebrating his discovery, Archimedes ran through the streets crying *heureka* ('I have found it'). This has given us the word 'eureka', expressing happiness and achievement.

Archimedes also studied the way a well-placed lever could shift a heavy weight and is supposed to have boasted: 'Give me a place to stand and I will move the Earth.' Also in the field of mechanics he invented a device for drawing water upwards which is still in use. Known as the Archimedes screw, it uses a giant rotating screw to draw water up inside a long cylinder.

Archimedes was killed at the fall of Syracuse by a Roman soldier who became annoyed that he seemed interested only in solving a problem in geometry using circles he had drawn in the sand.

Architecture

Greek designs in building are perhaps the most familiar legacy of ancient Greece because they have so often been imitated in the modern age. The British Museum in London and the General Post Office in New York are among the many famous buildings that copy the design of Greek **temples**. Original Greek temples and other stone buildings still stand, some better preserved than others, but anything made of wood has long since perished. One of the greatest surviving examples of Greek architecture is the **Parthenon** temple on the Acropolis in **Athens**.

The first stone temples were built in the 7th century BC. Later they developed the basic design of a rectangular space, to house the statue of a god, enclosed on all four sides by columns supporting a downwards-sloping tiled roof. The triangular front and back of the roof – the pediments – carried carved images and sculptures.

The basic building design remained

The *'**Archimedes** screw'*, named after the Greek mathematician and inventor. When the handle is turned, the large spiral screw pushes water from the lower to a higher elevation.

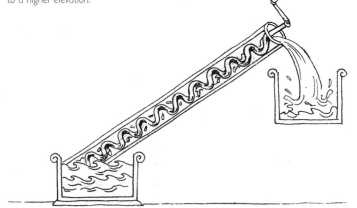

unchanged, though three different styles of columns developed in different parts of the Greek world: the Doric, the Ionian and the Corinthian. You can see examples of these three types of columns in the pictures on the right. The fluting (vertical grooves) on Greek stone columns probably goes back to the time before stone buildings, when tree trunks were used as columns. Vertical lines would be left on the wooden trunks when the bark was stripped off.

Rows of columns, called colonnades, became popular in non-temple buildings while domestic architecture developed around the courtyard (see **houses**). Straight lines and rectangular shapes dominate Greek architecture, although **theatres** developed a curved form, and vaulted (arched) ceilings were used in some elaborate tombs.

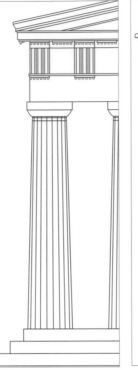

The DORIC order of column is sturdy with a plain capital. It was popular in mainland Greece.

The IONIC order is thinner and more graceful, and the capital is decorated with volutes, a spiral scroll design. This style was popular in **Asia Minor**.

The CORINTHIAN order has an elaborate capital, decorated with acanthus leaves and spiral scrolls. The first Corinthian capital appeared on the temple at **Bassae** *around 420 BC but it never became very common in Greek temples.*

The British Museum in London, with its Greek style of **architecture**: *a colonnade of Ionic columns and a pediment decorated with sculpted figures.*

Ariadne

In myth, Ariadne saved the life of **Theseus** by providing him with a ball of thread to unwind in the labyrinth so he could find his way out after killing the Minotaur, a bull-headed monster. She ran away with Theseus to escape her angry father, King **Minos** of Crete, but was betrayed and abandoned by Theseus on the island of Naxos (see map, page 62). She awoke on the island to see him sailing away.

In some versions of the story she died alone, but there is another, happier ending. **Dionysus** arrived on the scene, in a chariot drawn by panthers, and he and Ariadne married and had children. In another version, Theseus abandoned Ariadne only against his will and, because he was grieving for her, he forgot to change his sails to signal victory to his father, Aegeus. When Aegeus saw the black sails, he thought his son was dead and threw himself into the sea, which afterwards was called the Aegean.

Aristophanes

Aristophanes was a comic playwright in **Athens** who lived around 450–385 BC. Writing at the time when Athens was at war with **Sparta**, he often criticized the war politicians in his plays. In *Lysistrata*, written in 411, the women of Athens go on strike against their husbands until they agree to call for peace. In another of his plays, *Acharnians*, an Athenian farmer makes a private peace treaty with the Spartans while the war rages on about him. He attacks the contemporary philosopher **Socrates** in another play, *Clouds*, for being a dangerous crank.

Aristophanes seems to be opposed to many aspects of **democracy** in Athens, but he was also a product of its rich culture and spirit of inquiry. His plays discuss controversial issues, such as the role of women and the value of going to war, and performances of his work were very popular. Eleven of his plays have survived. They are the only complete comedies from 5th-century BC Greece.

*Below left: this painting by Titian, a 16th-century artist, is called Bacchus and **Ariadne**. Bacchus is another name for Dionysus.*

*Below right: a scene from the play Peace by **Aristophanes**, performed by modern actors in masks.*

Aristotle (Aristoteles)

A scientist, philosopher and teacher, Aristotle (384-322 BC) had an enormous influence on later thinkers. His work is recognized as one of the greatest expressions of ancient Greek thought.

He came from Stagirus, a Greek colony on the coast of Thrace, but settled in **Athens** at a young age and studied with **Plato** for twenty years. He came to reject Plato's idea that the everyday world of reality is only a pale shadow of perfect forms. Instead, Aristotle argued for the need to focus on the here-and-now. He established, for the first time, systems of classifying and describing the natural world. Aristotle left Athens after the death of Plato and set up his own school elsewhere, at one stage becoming a teacher to **Alexander the Great**.

In 335 BC he returned to Athens and established a school which became known as the Lyceum, a university of the ancient world. Aristotle created departments of study and directed research, wrote and lectured on subjects ranging from zoology to literature. He was over sixty when he fled Athens because of anti-Macedonian feelings. Referring to the death of **Socrates**, he said he was leaving to prevent the Athenians committing a second sin against philosophy.

When ancient Greece fell into decline, the eastern Mediterranean came under Arab influence. The works of Aristotle and others such as **Archimedes** were preserved by Arab scholars. In the 16th and 17th centuries, Aristotle's works were translated from Arabic into Latin, which was the language used by scholars all over Europe. European scholars could

A 16th-century painting by Raphael showing the famous philosophers of Athens. **Aristotle** *(centre right) points downwards to indicate his concern with everyday, down to earth matters.* **Plato** *(centre left) points upwards.*

then read the works of Aristotle and other ancient writers. This period of European history is known as the Renaissance (meaning 'rebirth') because of this rediscovery of ancient knowledge.

Armour and arms

We know about the early Greek armour and arms of the **Bronze Age** from descriptions of warriors in the poetry of **Homer**. A helmet and a large shield made of ox hide, which was supported from around the neck, provided the soldier's only defence against the enemy's swords and spears.

Later, during the **Classical Age**, the hoplite became the standard fighting man in any Greek army. He fought with a bronze shield and weapons made of iron. He was a **citizen** and a foot soldier. His standard armour consisted of a metal helmet, a protective breast-plate and back-plate made of linen or bronze, and greaves to protect his shins. He was armed with a sword, spear and shield.

Some hoplite units fought with thrusting spears 2 metres (7 feet) long. Others threw lighter spears against the enemy. The hoplites had to provide their armour and weapons themselves and they trained in local regiments. A hoplite's armour and weapons weighed around 25 kilograms (60 pounds), so a running battle could not be sustained for long.

Mercenaries were usually employed as general reinforcements though some of them had special fighting skills. Under **Alexander the Great** the phalanx, a compact formation of foot soldiers armed with spears of differing lengths, developed as a highly successful armoured fighting unit.

*Greek **armour**: a pair of greaves and a helmet from Corinth. They are made of bronze and were probably worn with a leather lining. The helmet weighs almost 1.5 kg (3 lbs) and the greaves over 0.5kg (1 lb) each.*

*Below: a Greek hoplite (soldier) with his **armour and arms**, ready to go to war. He says farewell to his father while his wife or mother waits with a bowl and some wine. When the bowl is filled with wine, some will be poured on the ground as an offering to the gods, and the remainder shared by the family as a final gesture of togetherness.*

Artemis

Artemis was the goddess of wild animals, the hunt and the wilderness but was also associated with women's lives. She was especially worshipped in Greek parts of Asia, where she merged with an Asiatic fertility goddess. The Temple of Artemis at Ephesus in **Asia Minor** was one of the Seven Wonders of the Ancient World. Artemis was also especially worshipped at **Sparta** and by the **Amazons**.

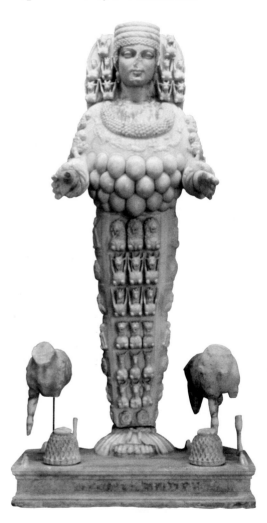

*The worship of **Artemis** is thought to have originated in Asia, and at Ephesus in **Asia Minor** a large temple was devoted to her. This statue of Artemis comes from Ephesus and indicates one of her roles as a goddess of fertility.*

The daughter of Leto, and twin sister of **Apollo**, Artemis is frequently pictured with a bow and arrow and in the company of wild animals. She was often seen as a violent and punishing deity. She caused the hunter Actaeon to be torn apart by his own hounds because he had seen her naked. She also slew the six daughters of Niobe, while Apollo killed the six sons, because their mother had boasted about the size of her family compared to Leto's two children. At **Troy**, **Agamemnon** was forced to sacrifice his daughter **Iphigenia** because he had earlier insulted Artemis.

Asclepius (Asklepios)

In legend, Asclepius was the son of the god **Apollo** by a human mother. He was instructed by a **Centaur** (a half-man, half-horse creature) in the art of **medicine**. His skill extended to being able to bring the dead back to life. The goddess **Artemis** persuaded Asclepius to use his skill on the dead mortal Hippolytus. However, **Zeus** saw this display of godlike power and sympathy for humans as a threat and he reacted by killing both Asclepius and Hippolytus with a thunderbolt.

***Asclepius** was worshipped throughout Greece and several healing shrines were dedicated to him. The centre of his cult worship was at Epidaurus and people came here hoping for a cure for their illnesses.*

Asclepius came to be widely worshipped as a god of healing and his major shrine was at Epidaurus (see map, page 62). By the end of the 5th century BC, pilgrims were visiting the shrine for its famed course of medicine. Pictures of Asclepius often show him with a staff and a snake coiled around it.

Asia Minor

The Aegean Sea and the narrow Bosporus strait separate Greece and the European mainland from the western coast of Asia Minor (now western Turkey). The story of the war at **Troy** may echo a time when Greeks first began to trade, make war and colonize this corner of their known world (see **colonies**).

The coast of western Asia Minor was on the Aegean and settlements began around 1000 BC in a region known as **Ionia**. The Greeks also colonized other coastal regions. Sometimes they replaced the non-Greek people; sometimes they lived peacefully alongside them, as with the people of **Caria**. Lycia, a region to the south-east, although strongly influenced by Greek culture, was mostly under Persian control until the time of **Alexander the Great**.

At the beginning of the 5th century BC, most of Asia Minor was governed by **Persia** through a system of regional governors. A failed rebellion against Persian rule by the Ionians led to the Persian invasion of Greece. After the defeat of the Persians, the Greek settlements in Asia Minor became part of the Delian League (see **Athenian Empire**). They were later handed back to Persia by **Sparta** in 386 BC. Alexander the Great invaded Asia Minor, defeating the Persians and liberating the Greek states, which once again became part of a larger Greek world.

Homer, **Herodotus** and **Thales** all came from Asia Minor, and Greek cities like **Miletus** played an important part in

Greeks first came to **Asia Minor** in search of trade. They were especially looking for metals such as tin, copper and gold. In Asia Minor they came into contact with eastern forms of art, which had an influence on the future development of Greek art.

Greek history and culture. Inland Asia Minor, however, remained largely a closed world to the Greeks. To them, it was part of the alien Persian Empire and was peopled by **barbarians**.

Assembly (Ekklesia)

The Assembly was a formal gathering of the male **citizens** of **Athens**. They met more than once every month for the business of government by **democracy**. The Assembly was also a court; it elected and sacked generals, it could banish citizens (see **ostracism**) and it debated proposals for new laws. Most decisions were made by a show of hands. The Assembly took place at the Pnyx, a hill near the **agora**. The exits from the agora were all closed during meetings except for one that led to the Pnyx. Armed Scythian slaves were on duty to keep order, and a rope with red dye was used to usher citizens from the agora to the Pnyx. Late attenders touched with the dye could be fined. A different chairman was elected each day by lot and there was a set agenda for each meeting. Any citizen could make a proposal by submitting it first to the elected Council that managed the business of the Assembly.

Athena (Athene)

The goddess Athena was the daughter of **Zeus** and a woman called Metis. A prophecy said that a son of Metis would threaten the gods, so Zeus swallowed Metis before she could give birth. Months later Zeus developed a terrible headache. In agony, he ordered **Hephaestus** to split his

*The birth of **Athena**. Her father, **Zeus**, holding his thunderbolt, sits on his throne decorated with a swan's head. **Hephaestus** stands to one side, holding the axe he used to open the head of Zeus.*

*An Athenian silver coin showing the owl of **Athena**.*

head open with an axe. Athena sprang out, already full-grown and in full armour.

Athena was a warrior goddess, but she was also the goddess of reason and the arts and was associated with peaceful activities like weaving. Athena had a reputation for wisdom and intelligence, symbolized by her favourite animal, the owl. Her shield carried an image of **Medusa**'s head, given to her by **Perseus**.

Athena was the patron goddess of **Athens** and gave the Athenian people the olive tree. They worshipped her in the **Panathenaea**. A huge statue of Athena stood in the **Parthenon**.

Athenian Empire

The Athenian Empire developed from the Delian League, which was formed in 478 BC as a defensive alliance against **Persia**. It began as an organization of equals. Representatives of the cities in **Asia Minor** joined those of the Aegean islands and Athens on the island of **Delos** (see map, page 62) to strengthen their defences against another attack. All the states contributed either money or ships. However, when the treasury was moved from Delos to Athens, it became clear that Athens wanted to control the states and turn the alliance into an empire.

Around 450 BC, the Persian threat had declined but, when some member states questioned the continuing need for a league, the Athenians used force to collect payments. The empire was broken up in 404 BC at the end of the **Peloponnesian War**, when Sparta defeated Athens.

Athens

Athens (see map, page 62) was the cultural capital of ancient Greece. We know more about Athens than any other part of the Greek world. A lot of evidence about ancient Greece comes in different ways from Athens. **Archaeology** has shown that there was a settlement on the **Acropolis** at Athens during the **Bronze Age**. It was Athenians (people of Athens) who first migrated to the coast of **Asia Minor** and founded the cities of **Ionia**.

In the late 6th century BC, **Solon** played a vital role in establishing a new constitution for Athens. The new constitution extended power to the rich as well as the nobles. A tyrant, Pisistratus, ruled the city for more than thirty years, but when he died, and after his son was expelled, political reforms turned Athens into a **democracy**.

Athens was involved in the **Persian Wars** but emerged victorious at the Battle of **Marathon** in 490 BC. An Athenian general, Themistocles, defeated the Persian fleet at **Salamis** in 480 BC. After these successes, an **Athenian Empire** developed, and under the statesman **Pericles** the city blossomed into a rich and exciting place for dramatists, artists and philosophers. Around 75,000 people lived in the city itself but the total population, including the surrounding area where **citizens** also lived, was some 250,000. There may have been twice as many **slaves** as citizens in Athens and the surrounding region, called Attica. Grain had to be imported (see **colonies**) to meet the demand for food.

The success of Athens worried other states including **Sparta** and **Corinth.** Their conflict led to the **Peloponnesian War**. A peace treaty was signed in 421 BC, after ten years of war, but peace did not last. Athens embarked on a disastrous invasion of **Sicily**, followed by nine more years of fighting Sparta. Athens was

*Modern **Athens**, with the **Parthenon** clearly visible on the Acropolis.*

defeated in 404 BC, after the destruction of its fleet, and its empire was finished. The end of the 5th century BC saw a weakening of democracy in Athens. More than once an **oligarchy** – government by a small group – was established. Athens remained important and was favourably treated under the rule of **Macedon** in the later 3rd century BC.

The cultural importance of Athens is enormous and far-reaching. In antiquity Athens was already so famous that the ancient Romans marvelled at its achievements and tried to imitate them. In the fields of **architecture**, **sculpture**, **philosophy**, history and **drama**, the influence and culture of Athens has lasted for well over two thousand years.

After the Persian Wars, the city of Athens was largely rebuilt. The main city was joined to the port of Piraeus by the 11-kilometre (7-mile) Long Walls (see page 115). Entering the city, visitors passed the Pnyx on their left, where the **Assembly** met, and found themselves in the **agora** at the heart of Athens, surrounded by **temples**, altars and buildings. A steep road led up to the Acropolis and the statue of **Athena** in the **Parthenon**.

Athletics

Greeks were proud of their love of athletics and competitive events. This was a tradition that went back to the heroic age described by **Homer**, and it is an aspect of Greek civilization that has had a big influence on our own times. Four major athletics competitions attracted participants from all over the Greek world, in particular the **Olympic Games** at Elis in the Peloponnese and the Pythian Games at **Delphi**.

Most athletes were professionals in the sense that they trained full-time, attended all or most of the athletic competitions and could expect substantial rewards if they won at a prestigious **competition** such as the Olympic Games. They came mostly from rich, aristocratic families as only members of that class could afford to devote so much time to athletics. Some athletes had their own coaches. Training took place mostly in the **gymnasium**, and athletes covered their bodies with olive oil to keep off the dust.

Athletes' diet consisted of lots of meat, which was unusual for most Greeks

*An **athletics** competition. Greek jumpers carried weights to help propel them forward at the start of the jump. On landing, as shown here, the weights were swung backwards to create a forward thrust. Onlookers applaud, impressed by the fact that the jump beats the previous attempts marked by pegs in the ground.*

(see **food**). Some Greek writers criticized athletes for their unnatural diet, for being obsessed with sport, and for the great wealth that champions could accumulate.

The main events were running, javelin-throwing, **wrestling**, **boxing** and **chariot racing**. The pentathlon consisted of the long-jump, running, javelin, wrestling and **discus**. There were no team events and no keeping of records. The object of the competition was to achieve an individual victory and the rules were pushed to the limit by athletes in their determination to win. There were prizes for the winners, but being a runner-up counted for nothing.

Athenian victors received free meals for life in the city's town hall, and poets were commissioned by some of the proud victors to compose odes in their honour. The odes would be sung as part of a civic reception held to honour a victorious athlete. Some of these odes, written by Pindar in the 5th century BC, have survived. It would have cost a lot of money to commission a famous poet like Pindar.

Atlantis

In legend, Atlantis was an island in the Atlantic Ocean that flourished in the far distant past, went to war against **Athens**

*Four men ready to take part in **athletics**. From left to right: a jumper holding his jumping-weights; a javelin-thrower poised ready to throw; a discus-thrower with a discus in his hand; and another javelin-thrower holding his javelin.*

and was eventually destroyed by a vast flood. The myth is told by **Plato**, who added to the legend a fanciful account of how a succession of semi-divine kings ruled the island. The tale of Atlantis may be based on a memory of the destruction of the island of Thera by volcanic eruptions between 1650 and 1500 BC.

Atlas

Atlas was a giant who had to hold the sky on his shoulder as a punishment from **Zeus**. He was one of the Titans (see **creation myth**) who had been on the losing side in the struggle between the old divinities and the new order of gods. He carried out his task in the far west, at the edge of the sea, in the land of the Hesperides where **Heracles** was sent on one of his labours. Atlas offered to fetch the golden apples that Heracles sought if Heracles would take the burden of the sky off him while he did so. Atlas intended to leave Heracles holding up the sky, but the hero tricked him into taking it back on his shoulders again.

*This marble sculpture dates to the 3rd century AD and is from the Indian subcontinent. It shows an **Atlas**-like figure holding up the sky on his shoulders, suggesting that the myth of Atlas travelled far beyond the Greek homeland.*

B

A famous story told how the hero **Heracles** strangled two snakes that attacked him in his **babyhood**.

Babyhood

Babyhood could be a dangerous time in ancient Greece. At birth some unwanted babies were abandoned and left to die from exposure away from the home. It is not known how widespread this practice was. Girls were far more likely to be abandoned than boys because ancient Greece was very much a man's world. Also, girls were more expensive because a family had to provide a dowry for a girl when she got married (see **marriage**). Deformed or sickly babies and babies born to slaves were also at risk.

Babies that were not exposed faced a high possibility of dying through disease or illness, as infants still do in many parts of the world. Probably as many as one in four babies died during their first year. Upper-class families regularly hired nurses to feed and look after their infants. There were festivals when babies born to citizens were registered, and in Athens three- and four-year-olds took part in a spring festival and tasted wine for the first time. It is not known, however, if girls took part in any of these festivals. (See also **childhood**.)

Barbarians

Although they spent a lot of time fighting one another, the Greeks had a keen sense of their own identity. They called anyone who was not Greek a 'barbarian'. This word captured what to the Greeks was the meaningless noise ('bar-bar') of any language spoken by foreigners.

Such an attitude towards non-Greeks was not evident in the time of **Homer**. However, by the 5th century BC, after the experience of confronting a non-Greek enemy in **Persia**, Greeks saw 'barbarians' as a type. They were people with no sense of political or moral freedom, strangers who spoke, dressed and thought differently and so could not be Greek.

Bassae

Bassae lies high up in the spectacular mountain region of Arcadia in the Peloponnese. The temple to **Apollo** built there around 450 BC was the first temple to use Corinthian columns (see **architecture**). The sculpted frieze portrayed **Heracles** and other Greeks battling with **barbarians**, **Amazons** and **Centaurs**. An expedition from Europe in the 19th century AD removed the frieze. It was sold to the British government and is now in the British Museum in London.

A mother holds out her arms to her baby. She has a piece of fruit in her hand.

*Civilization versus the **barbarians** was a popular theme in Greek art. This sculptured scene, which once decorated the Temple of Apollo at **Bassae**, depicts a battle of **Heracles** (centre) and other Greeks against the **Amazons**. A fallen Greek is on the left while on the right an Amazon is unseated from her horse.*

Boxing

Boxing was a highly-esteemed event in Greek **athletics** competitions. The ancient sport had some different rules from modern boxing. There were referees but there was no ring. There were no rounds and no weight divisions. Contestants boxed until one of them was unable to continue or gave up the fight by raising his index finger. Blows could be delivered with the fist or the open hand. Gouging (thumbing in the eyes) was forbidden but kicking was allowed. Boxers did not wear boxing gloves. Their fingers were wrapped separately in pieces of leather like bandages, for protection.

*Below left: A boxer is making an adjustment to the thongs of his **boxing** glove. The thong goes some way up the forearm and strips of sheepskin could be added around the forearm, acting like the sweatbands that some modern athletes use.*

Bronze Age

The Bronze Age is the name of the period between roughly 3000 and 1000 BC. It followed the Neolithic, or New Stone Age. The Bronze Age takes its name from the newly discovered technique of making bronze from copper and tin. Tools for agriculture and weapons for war made from bronze were superior to anything that had gone before. However, tin was not plentiful in Greece and supplies depended on overseas trade. Bronze weapons and tools were mostly for the powerful and the rich.

The Bronze Age in Greece came to an end when the technique of forging iron was discovered, shortly after 1000 BC. There was a plentiful supply of iron and so poorer people could afford iron tools and weapons.

The heroic world recorded by **Homer** was a Bronze Age society. So were the **Minoan civilization** of **Crete** and the **Mycenaean civilization**.

*A **Bronze Age** dagger from Mycenae.*

C

Calypso (Kalypso)

The **nymph** Calypso lived on the island of Ogygia. **Odysseus** was washed ashore on the island while sailing home from **Troy**. He remained with Calypso for seven years and she promised him immortality if he stayed, but Odysseus wanted to return home to his wife and son. At **Athena**'s request, the messenger-god **Hermes** was sent to Calypso with orders from **Zeus** to let Odysseus go. She reluctantly agreed, and helped Odysseus make a raft. She gave him food and advice on how to navigate homewards.

Caria

Caria was a region (see map, page 23) in the southwest of **Asia Minor.** Caria came under Greek influence, though not as strongly as **Ionia**, its neighbour. The historian **Herodotus** came from the city of Halicarnassus in Caria. When Asia Minor was part of the empire ruled by **Persia**, a Carian called Skylax of Karyanda travelled east to explore the Indus and a route to the Red Sea. The myth of **Endymion** is associated with Caria.

The most famous building in Halicarnassus was a monumental tomb, built to glorify the ruler Mausolus. Known as the Mausoleum, it was one of the Seven Wonders of the Ancient World.

Cassandra

Cassandra was the most beautiful of the daughters of Priam, the king of **Troy**. She was pursued by the god **Apollo**, who promised her the gift of prophecy in return for her love. She accepted the gift, but spurned him. Apollo retaliated by giving her the power of prophecy but making sure that no one would ever believe her.

No one believed her prediction that the return of **Paris** to Troy with **Helen** would lead to the destruction of Troy. She warned everyone that the **Wooden Horse**

*The word 'mausoleum' means a large and grand tomb. It comes from 'Mausolus', the name of a king whose splendid tomb at Halicarnassus in **Caria** became famous in the ancient world. Only the foundations and some of the tomb's sculptures now remain, but this artist's reconstruction gives some idea of how dramatic it must have looked.*

*This black-figure cup shows a Greek warrior, known as the Lesser **Ajax**, dragging **Cassandra** from her hiding-place behind a statue of **Athena**.*

was full of Greek warriors but once again no one believed her.

After Troy was destroyed, **Agamemnon** brought Cassandra back with him to Mycenae as his slave. She was murdered along with Agamemnon by his wife, Clytemnestra. Cassandra knew this would happen but also knew that she would not be able to convince anybody of the truth.

Cavalry

The **geography of Greece** never encouraged the large-scale use of horses in warfare. It was too difficult to move numbers of mounted men around in the steep, mountainous terrain. It was also expensive to keep horses unless the owner had plenty of grazing land (see **farming**). Citizens had to pay for their own armour and only the very rich could afford the extra expense of horses, so that the cavalry in a Greek army was

usually small. Being a Greek cavalryman was very prestigious, even though mounted fighters rarely played a crucial role in battle. **Alexander the Great** developed the role of the cavalry and used it to attack in force after the phalanx (the infantry formation) had engaged the enemy.

Centaurs

A Centaur was a mythical creature, half man and half horse. Centaurs were a favourite topic in Greek art. They were usually portrayed in **myth** as wild and uncivilized, living in wild regions such as **Thessaly** and Arcadia, and behaving like beasts.

Homer tells of a mighty battle between Centaurs and a people from Thessaly called the Lapiths. **Heracles** battled with Centaurs more than once. There was one civilized Centaur, Chiron, who was the wise tutor to **Achilles**.

*This red figure plate shows an armed man, perhaps a **cavalry**-man, with his horse.*

*Some of the **Parthenon** sculptures show a fierce battle between **Centaurs** and Lapiths. In this scene, the Centaur seems to be winning, but the battle as a whole resulted in the defeat of the barbarian half-man and half-horse creatures.*

Chariot Races

Chariots were used in **warfare** in Mycenaean times, but by the **Classical Age** they were used only in sport. Chariot racing traditionally took place at the **Olympic Games**. There is a record of one race in which more than forty chariots took part. At Olympia a chariot race consisted of twelve laps of almost 1,000 metres (1,100 yards) each, so the total distance was some 12 kilometres (8 miles).

A single charioteer had four horses to pull his two-wheeled chariot. There was plenty of scope for accidents and collisions. In the race involving over forty chariots, the winner was the only charioteer who managed to survive the multiple crashes and finish the race. Not surprisingly, chariot races were the highlight of sporting festivals.

*Scenes from a coin (above) and a pot (below) showing a charioteer steering his four horses. A winged **Nike** (Victory) hovers over the chariot on the coin. The chariots were made of wood and had no springs. Given the dangers of **chariot races**, most owners of horses and chariots employed someone else to drive them.*

Charon

Charon was the mythical boatman who supervised the passage of the dead across the river Styx to the Underworld. He collected the payment of one obol (see **funerals**).

Charon steered the boat, which was rowed by the shades of the dead. He was noted for his rudeness. He at first refused to take **Heracles** across until Heracles forced him. Afterwards the gods punished Charon for allowing a human to enter the Underworld.

*The Greeks sometimes placed a coin in the mouth of the corpse so that **Charon** could be paid for the journey to Hades. This is what the artist John Stanhope is referring to in this 19th-century AD painting.*

Childhood

Once past **babyhood**, children had their own important parts to play in festivals and religious rituals. They took part in choral singing and dancing. Girls had special responsibilities, like grinding the corn for cakes used in rituals for **Athena** or **Demeter**. Boys joined the musical and athletic competitions that accompanied some of the more important festivals.

Education was usually very different

*Left: a clay dancing doll, with moveable arms and legs, holding a form of castanet in one hand. There were various **toys and games** for the amusement of young children.*

*Below: a scene of **childhood**: a child crawling towards its mother.*

for boys and girls. This reflected the fact that boys were seen as more important than girls. It was boys who inherited property and looked after their parents when they grew old.

Chorus

The chorus, consisting of some fifteen trained men, played a major part in Greek **drama**. The chorus danced in an area in front of the stage called the **orchestra** and at the same time they sang elaborate odes concerning the action of the play.

Circe

Circe was a witch, who played an important part in the return of **Odysseus** from **Troy**. When he landed on Circe's island (which was probably in Italy), Odysseus sent half his men out to explore. They found a palace and went in, leaving only Eurylochus on guard. He watched how Circe changed all the men into pigs and herded them into a sty. Then he rushed back to warn Odysseus,

*Below, In this 16th-century AD painting by Dosso Dossi, **Circe** is surrounded by animals and birds. They are humans she has magically transformed.*

33

who set out to rescue them. On his way Odysseus met **Hermes**, who gave him the magical herb moly to counteract Circe's magic. Using the herb, Odysseus was able to force the witch to restore his men. Odysseus lived with Circe for a year before leaving for home.

Citizens

Greek citizens thought of themselves as members of a **city-state**, or *polis* as the Greeks called it. Every citizen was proud to have the honour of citizenship. Male citizens were members of the **Assembly** and could take part in deciding the laws of the polis. Slaves were scarcely ever allowed to become citizens. Free women had few of the rights of male citizens. Male citizens had to fight in defence of the polis.

The history of **democracy** in **Athens** records the gradual widening of eligibility for citizenship. By the 5th century BC, every free adult male whose parents were citizens had this right and was therefore a member of the Assembly.

In other city-states, citizenship was often restricted to the property-owning rich or to those who could prove descent from a known or a legendary founder (see **oligarchy**). Proof of parenthood was a vital matter. Even in Athens it was a strict condition of citizenship that one's father and mother were both free citizens, and this had to be established at the age of eighteen. Out of the 250,000 people living in Athens, only about 40,000 were citizens.

City-state (Polis)

'City-state' is the meaning of the ancient Greek word *polis*. This described the form of society that most Greeks felt they shared, and that helped create their sense of a common culture. The polis included the town and the surrounding

*The island **city-state** of Aegina chose a sea creature, a turtle, for its emblem. It is shown here on a coin.*

country, where most of the people lived. It would be wrong to think that the Greeks lived only in cities (see **farming**). The many city-states of ancient Greece had lots of different types of government: from **democracies** to **oligarchies** and kingdoms. Whatever form a government took, the polis always covered a particular geographical area in which all citizens felt strong ties of community. The city-state of **Athens** occupied about 2,600 square kilometres (1,000 square miles) but many city-states were much smaller.

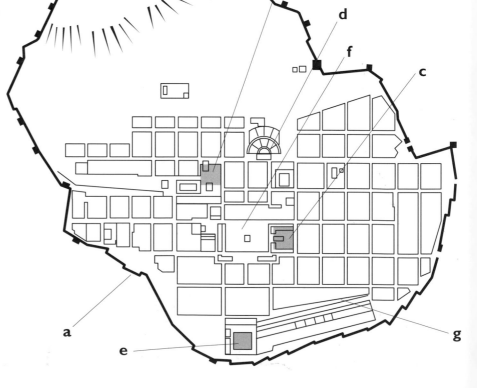

*A plan of Priene in Asia Minor showing the typical features of a **city-state**. The city was built on the slopes of a hill below an **acropolis** and surrounded by walls (a). There were two **temples** (b) and (c), a **theatre** (d), a **gymnasium** (e), an **agora** (f) and a **stadium** (g).*

Classical Age

The **history of Greece** falls into different periods. The Classical Age is the name given to most of the 5th and 4th centuries BC. It started around 480 BC, when the Greeks defeated **Persia**, and ended in 323 BC with the death of **Alexander the Great**. It was the period when Greek culture was at its richest and the city of **Athens** was very much at the centre of cultural and political events.

We know a lot about the Classical Age because later Greek scholars (of the 3rd–1st centuries BC) preserved and copied documents and literature from that period. Later still, ancient **Rome** came under the influence of Greek culture. Through their writings and art the Romans influenced European learning during the Renaissance and after.

*A sculpted bronze head of the god **Apollo** from the **Classical Age**. Classical sculptors were famous for their skill in creating images of idealized human beauty.*

*Below: the remains of the east front of the **Parthenon**, one of the most impressive buildings of the **Classical Age**.*

Climate

The climate of Greece has hot dry summers, cool winters and varying amounts of rainfall. It starts becoming warm in April, crops are ripe before June and little rain falls between mid-June and mid-September.

Farming was precarious in the past. There was always the danger of food shortages when not enough rain fell to water the crops. Droughts and famine often occurred and life could be unpredictable. The absence of really cold weather, and the rarity of rain during the summer, encouraged an outdoor life. **Theatres** were always outdoors, as were meetings of the **Assembly**. The climate also influenced the **clothes** that people wore.

*Below: a hot and cloudless day in southern Greece, typical of the Greek **climate**.*

Clocks

*Above: an Egyptian water **clock**. The water poured out of the pot through a hole at the bottom and as the level fell markers inside the pot showed how much time had passed. The Greeks knew about these clocks and used them.*

The Greeks did not have mechanical clocks as we know them, but they had ways of measuring the passing of time. The Greeks adopted the sundial and the water clock, which were known to the ancient Egyptians and Babylonians. A water clock measured how long it took for a certain quantity of water to pass from one container to another. The water clock was used in **Athens** to measure the length of time allowed for speeches in court. The vast majority of people did not need clocks and could roughly tell the time of day from the position of the sun. Farmers also used the appearance and positions of some stars as a kind of agricultural calendar.

*Left: a fragment of an Egyptian klepsydra (water **clock**).*

Clothes

Most clothes were of finely spun wool or flax and were made at home, usually by women. Colour was added to clothing by the use of natural dyes from plants and animals. Saffron yellow was a favourite colour among women while dark colours were worn for mourning. The most expensive colour was purple, because the dye had to be extracted from the murex shellfish by a costly process.

Better-off people could afford finer materials such as silk. Poorer people could hardly even afford to dye their woollen garments. The basic item of clothing, worn by men and women, was the *chiton*. This consisted of a single piece of cloth folded into two halves at the top, where it was fastened over the body with brooches or pins. It was gathered in at the waist by a belt and could reach to the ground or be pulled up over the belt for greater ease of movement when working. The *peplos* was a similar, loose-fitting garment but it was sleeveless.

When the temperature dropped, a cloak called a *himation* was worn over the shoulders. The *chlamys* was a special kind of himation which could be worn over one shoulder and fastened on the other side, or worn over both shoulders and fastened at the throat. In bright sunshine men often wore a wide-brimmed hat called a *petasos*. Underwear may not have been very common. It was not fitted, but worn as a wrap-around under the chiton.

Shoes and sandals were made of leather but many people probably went barefoot. This was partly because of the warm climate but also because most people were too poor to afford footwear.

Above, *a woman adjusting the belt of her* chiton. *The top edges are joined with pins.*

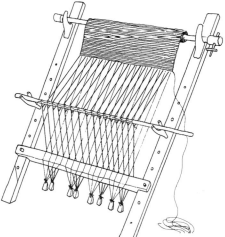

Right: women made the family's **clothes** *at home. They wove cloth on looms like this one.*

This white-ground jug shows a woman wearing a chiton *and spinning thread on a distaff.*

Below: a woman is putting a chiton over her head. A strip of cloth serves as a bra.

Below: a man wearing a chlamys *fastened on one shoulder and a* petasos *(hat).*

Coins

The first coins were made by non-Greeks in **Lydia**, in **Asia Minor**, around 600 BC. Earlier, the Greeks had traded using silver or iron pieces. The Lydians made their coins out of electrum, a mixture of gold and silver. When the Greeks began to mint coins, they used silver or gold, and later some bronze was also used. **Athens** and **Corinth**, which both engaged in overseas trading, were among the first cities to issue their own coins.

At first coins were stamped on one side only, with a special mark to show they contained a fixed amount of silver. Later, coins were stamped on both sides and carried emblems or mythological figures. Each city minted its own coins, which, as a mark of civic pride, were often very beautiful. Athenian coins usually carried an image of the owl, a symbol of the city's goddess, **Athena**. Money changers exchanged one city's coinage for another. **Sparta** never developed a coinage. (See also **money**.)

*Two sides of a four-drachma silver **coin** from Athens. The coin was worth about four days' pay for a skilled craftsman.*

*The location of Greek **colonies** was influenced by the availability of much-needed resources. Grain came from the Black Sea area, from north **Africa**, and from **Egypt**. Egypt also supplied flax and papyrus. Textiles and metals came from **Phoenicia**.*

Colonies

Some Greeks left mainland Greece in search of trade and raw materials, especially metal. They first colonized **Ionia**, with its fertile plains and great river valleys, and Cyprus. Later, from around 700 BC until about 550 BC, an increase in population and shortages of food led many mainland Greeks to emigrate to southern **Italy**, **Sicily**, **Thrace** and the Black Sea area. The Black Sea area was a valuable source of grain. Protecting the sea route there was of vital importance, especially to **Athens**. The Greeks colonized nearly all of the coast of **Asia Minor** as well as Libya. In the west, settlements were established at Massilia (modern Marseilles in France) and in southern Spain.

When a colony was established, the first settlers kept close political and economic ties with their home state. The government of the new **city-state**, or *polis*, was founded along the same lines as those of the mother city, the *metropolis*

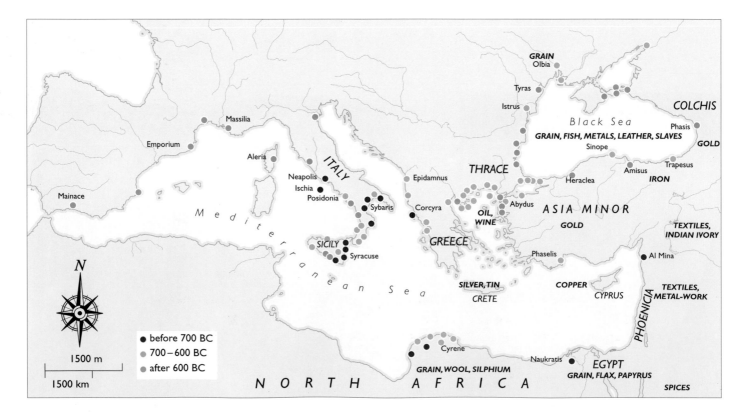

(from *meter*, Greek for 'mother'). More emigrants could be invited to join the colony and farm the land. Often conflicts arose between the settlers and the non-Greeks already living there. Occasionally, as in the case of **Corinth**, there was disagreement between the colonists and the mother city. Sometimes a colony was little more than a military garrison, especially under **Alexander the Great**, for example, Al Kanoum in what is now Afghanistan.

Competition

Ancient Greek society was intensely competitive. To a **citizen** of one of the Greek **city-states** it was important to prove that you were better than others. The worst thing was to have other people's disapproval, which brought **shame** on yourself and your family. Helping friends (who in turn offered their help to you) and harming enemies was part of the competitive attitude. People occasionally used **magic** to gain honour or bring shame on someone else.

In the **Iliad**, Achilles' father tells him 'always to be the best and excel over others'. The great plays of Greek **drama** were performed at sponsored competitions and there were four major competitive events for **athletics**, as well as musical competitions. In sports events no performance records were kept. The distance a javelin was thrown or the best time for a race was not important. All that mattered was winning the event.

A competitive spirit also affected everyday behaviour and, perhaps because life was hard and the power of community was strong, society judged success in competitive terms. In **law courts**, winning an argument about what had happened was often more important than questions about who was right or wrong.

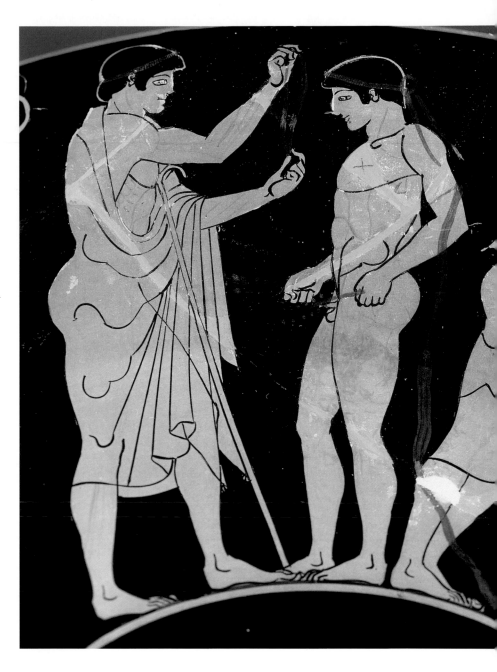

*Winning was everything. The picture on this drinking cup shows the winner of an athletics **competition** receiving a token of victory. It could be branches of palm or, in this case, woollen ribbons which were tied around the head, arms or legs.*

Cooking

Most cooking took place out in the open because of the warm, dry **climate**. A cooking pot was suspended over a fire using a chain, or metal bars were laid over the fire to support the cooking vessel. In a household, the woman was

Cooking in ancient Greece. This terracotta figure shows a woman baking bread in a low, domed clay oven. Poorer families would cook their bread in an earthenware pot with a lid, hung over an open fire.

century BC, Corinth had a population of about 90,000. Corinthian **colonies** were established in **Sicily**, on the island of Corcyra (modern Corfu) and elsewhere. The colony at Corcyra quarrelled with Corinth and rebelled. Corinth's aristocratic government was overthrown around 657 BC. A tyrant (a leader who seized power) called Cypselus took control. His son, Periander, also became a tyrant. After Periander's death, around 585 BC, an **oligarchy** (government by a few people) was established. It lasted nearly until the time Corinth came under the rule of **Macedon**.

Corinth and **Athens** had been on friendly terms and fought together against **Persia** in 480 BC. The development of the **Athenian Empire**, however, caused alarm in Corinth, especially when Corinth's former colony, Corcyra, made a treaty with Athens. This led to the **Peloponnesian War**. Later, Corinth fought alongside Athens against **Sparta** in what became known as the Corinthian War (395–386 BC).

The site of the ancient city state of **Corinth**, *which was destroyed by the Romans in 146 BC. Corinth once dominated the isthmus it stood on.*

responsible for meals but, unless the family was poor, **slaves** did the cooking and washing up. There were utensils to help in the cooking but people did not use knives and forks at meals. They ate with their fingers.

The hot climate made the preservation of **food** very difficult. Pickling was used as a way of keeping some foods edible. Some fish and meat were dried, smoked or salted to help preserve them.

Corinth

Corinth (see map, page 62) developed in the 7th and 6th centuries BC as a major trading port and a commercial centre. Its pottery was exported around the Greek world, especially to Italy. By the 5th

Creation Myth

The earliest gods were the Titans. Cronus, who was a Titan, became their ruler after he deposed his father and married his sister, Rhea. A prophecy warned Cronus that his own children would depose him, so he swallowed each of them as they were born. But when **Zeus** was born, Rhea tricked Cronus by giving him a stone wrapped in baby clothes.

Zeus grew up and deposed his father as the prophecy had said. Cronus had to vomit up his other children. The sons of Cronus divided up the world among them: Zeus ruled the sky, **Poseidon** the sea, and **Hades** the world of the dead (the Underworld). Zeus imprisoned Cronus and the other Titans in Tartarus, the lowest level of the Underworld.

Crete

The largest island in the Aegean Sea, Crete (see map, page 62) was the home of the **Minoan civilization** in the **Bronze Age**. The Minoans were the founders of

the earliest advanced society in Europe, which developed around 2200 BC. They were not Greeks but they had a vital influence on **Mycenaean civilization**.

The largest settlement of Minoan Crete was **Knossos**. In 1900 the archaeologist Arthur Evans excavated there and found a palace that had flourished around 1700 BC. He also discovered that, by 1400 BC, all the buildings on Crete had been destroyed by fire, caused by Greeks from the mainland. Centuries later, Crete was colonized by Greeks.

Croesus (Kroisos)

Croesus was the last king of **Lydia** in **Asia Minor**. He ruled from around 560 to 546 BC, when his country was conquered by **Persia**. Croesus was famous for his

*Below right: **Croesus** on top of the funeral fire where he was about to be burned. Legend has it that he was miraculously saved by **Apollo**.*

*Below left: This bronze figure shows a boy somersaulting over the horns of a bull. The **Minoan civilization** of **Crete** regarded the bull as a sacred animal. A form of bullfighting or bull-leaping seems to have been practised on Crete.*

wealth. As king he was friendly towards Greece, which lay to the west of his kingdom, but he wanted to expand eastwards into Persia. This met with resistance from the Persians, who captured his city and took him prisoner.

The great wealth and power of Croesus, and then his sudden fall from prosperity, illustrated the Greek idea of **hubris** – the sense that life is unpredictable and that pride can always lead to disaster. Before Croesus attacked Persia, he sought the advice of the oracle at **Delphi**. The oracle told him that if he advanced against Persia a mighty empire would be brought down. It never occurred to him that the oracle might be referring to the fall of his own kingdom. The downfall of Croesus was the consequence of his hubris. The Greeks called this downfall **nemesis** – divine vengeance.

Cronus (Kronos)

A Titan, the father of **Zeus** in the **creation myth**.

Cyclopes

The Cyclopes were a mythical race of savage, one-eyed giants who herded sheep in a land far away from Greece where there were no laws or cities. The most famous Cyclops was Polyphemus.

On his way home from the **Trojan War**, the hero **Odysseus** landed his ship in the Cyclopes' territory and took twelve of his men into Polyphemus's cave in search of food. While they were inside, the giant returned and closed the cave entrance with a huge rock. He discovered the men and asked Odysseus who he was. Odysseus answered, 'My name is Nobody.' Polyphemus began to eat the men, two at a time, until Odysseus made the giant drunk with wine. He fell asleep and Odysseus heated a sharpened post in the fire and blinded him.

Hearing his cries, other Cyclopes came to the cave entrance and asked him who was hurting him. He called out,'Nobody', and so the other Cyclopes left. Next day, Polyphemus opened the cave entrance and sat in the doorway, hoping to catch the men as they tried to escape. But they managed to sneak past him tied on to the underbellies of his sheep as they went out to graze. Polyphemus called on his father, the god **Poseidon**, for revenge. From then on, Poseidon worked against Odysseus until he reached home.

In another legend, the Cyclopes were master-blacksmiths who lived with the gods and provided **Zeus** with lightning and thunderbolts to help defeat the old race of gods, the Titans.

*Polyphemus, one of the **Cyclopes**, sits dazed and blinded as **Odysseus** escapes from his cave by hanging from the underbelly of a sheep.*

D

Daedalus and Icarus
(Daidalos and Ikaros)

Daedalus was a legendary inventor and artist who lived in Athens. He had a nephew who was also an inventor. His nephew invented the saw, after watching the way the jaws of a serpent worked. Daedalus became madly jealous and he killed his nephew by throwing him from the top of the **Acropolis**. Afterwards Daedalus fled to Crete, where he worked for King **Minos**. He was imprisoned by Minos in a tower because he had helped Minos' wife, who was in love with a bull. This union led to the birth of the Minotaur, a monster that was half man, half bull. Daedalus then designed a labyrinth to hold the Minotaur. In his prison tower Daedalus made wings of wax and feathers for himself and his son, Icarus, so that they could escape from Crete. Daedalus warned Icarus not to fly too near the sun because his wings would melt. Icarus did not listen to his father's advice. He flew too close to the sun, the wax holding his wings together melted, and he fell to his death.

*A 16th-century AD painting by Breughel the Elder giving an unusual view of the myth of **Daedalus and Icarus**. People go about their daily work as Icarus falls, unnoticed, into the sea (look to the right of the picture, in front of the ship.)*

Delos

A small island in the Aegean Sea, where Leto gave birth to **Apollo** and **Artemis**, the twin children of **Zeus**. The Greeks believed that Delos was originally a floating island. Leto was persecuted by **Hera**, the jealous wife of Zeus. She fled until she could find somewhere not on solid ground to give birth. The holy island became the greatest religious centre of the Greek peoples of Ionia.

The Delian League, which grew into the **Athenian Empire**, had its first headquarters on Delos.

Delphi

Delphi (see map, page 62) was the site of the most important shrine and **oracle** anywhere in the Greek world. According to legend, **Zeus** decided to create an oracle and sanctuary dedicated to his son **Apollo** and so he sent two eagles flying around the world in opposite directions. Where they met he founded the oracle. This spot was the navel of the earth, its central point, and was known to the Greeks as the *omphalos*

*The remains at **Delphi** of a circular building called a tholos, with three of its surrounding columns still standing. It stood inside the sanctuary to the goddess Athena.*

The myth says that, before the shrine at Delphi could be built, Apollo had to kill a serpent, the Pytho, that protected the site. To archaeologists and ancient historians, this story suggests that there may have been a temple to an earlier religion at Delphi before the Greeks made it a temple to Apollo.

Many people travelled to Delphi to consult the oracle, and every four years the Pythian Games were held there (see **athletics**). The most famous of the proverbs inscribed around the temple were 'Know Thyself' and 'Nothing in Excess'. The Athenians built a treasury at Delphi to store the valuable gifts presented to the temple to mark their victory at **Marathon**. Many other cities also consulted the oracle, especially when a new colony was being planned.

The oracle at Delphi was of major political importance. Rich and powerful men came here or sent their messengers to receive the words of the god. During three months of the year when Apollo was absent, **Dionysus** was believed to inhabit the shrine.

The ruins of a temple still stand at Delphi, on a terraced platform of rock high above the sea. These ruins date back to the early 4th century BC. An even older temple that stood on the site was destroyed by an earthquake.

Demeter and Persephone

Demeter was the goddess of corn and agriculture. Her name comes from *meter*, the Greek for 'mother'. One day, her daughter Persephone was out walking and collecting flowers when she was kidnapped by **Hades**, the god of the Underworld, who took her down to his kingdom as his wife. Demeter almost

Demeter and Persephone. Demeter is on the left, holding a burning torch and stalks of corn. She is about to offer them to Triptolemos, who is seated on the winged chariot. According to legend, Demeter taught the human Triptolemos how to grow corn. Persephone is on the right.

went mad with despair searching for her lost daughter. She would not eat and, because she controlled **farming** and the fertility of the land, nothing would grow. The world was in a state of perpetual winter.

Finally, **Zeus** took pity on Demeter and made Hades release Persephone. However, because she had eaten some pomegranate seeds in the Underworld, she could not be released completely. Persephone had to spend the winter of every year in the Underworld, returning each spring with fresh flowers to signal her reunion with her mother and the return of fruitfulness to the earth.

Festivals associated with Demeter celebrated her powers of fertility. They included the women-only **Thesmophoria** as well as the **Eleusinian Mysteries**. Shrines to Demeter spread across all of the Greek world. Many of them were said to be places where the goddess was befriended by local people as she searched for her daughter. In return for the kindness they showed her, Demeter taught people the arts of agriculture.

Democracy

Democracy is the form of **government** developed at **Athens** under Cleisthenes and others. The word comes from two Greek words: *demos* ('people') and *kratos* ('rule') and means rule by the people. Democracy was based on the principle that all the **citizens** of the **city-state** of Athens had the right to attend and speak at the **Assembly**. They could help to pass laws and decide how Athens would deal with other city-states.

Athenian democracy was not like modern democracies, where people elect representatives to sit in parliament and make the laws for them. Most government officers were chosen by lottery. Whoever was chosen did the job for one year with pay. Jurors for the **law courts** were selected in the same way. After 390 BC, citizens were paid just for attending the Assembly. The most important political posts were the *strategoi*, the ten generals. These men were elected by the Assembly each year.

There were somewhere between 30,000 and 40,000 male Athenian citizens. Only about 5,000 attended the Assembly and probably only a small number of these spoke regularly. Public speaking skills, a loud voice and lots of confidence were required. Everyone had the right to vote, usually by a show of hands. However, the vote for an **ostracism** (banishment from Athens) was handled differently.

Athenian democracy did not extend to **women**, **slaves** and foreign residents.

Dionysia

The Dionysia was a festival that took its name from the god **Dionysus**. It was celebrated in Athens each year at the end of March to mark the return of Spring to the countryside. It was a major holiday for Athenians, lasting for a week. Even slaves were given time off work to join in the festivities. Processions took place through the city and special performances of plays (see **drama**) took place in the Theatre of Dionysus, which was close to the god's shrine.

*The pot shows the bearded god **Dionysus** with a **satyr** who has the tail and ears of a horse. During the **Dionysia**, satyr plays were often performed.*

Dionysus (Dionysos)

The most exciting of the Greek gods was Dionysus. His image was more popular in Greek art than that of any other deity. Dionysus was the god of wine and he was often associated with **satyrs**. He stood for a spirit of joyful anarchism that opposed the reason and order represented by **Apollo**.

Dionysus was the son of the god **Zeus** but his mother, Semele, was human. When **Hera**, the wife of Zeus, heard that Semele was having Zeus' baby, she grew very angry and jealous. She decided to take revenge on Semele. Hera tricked Semele into asking Zeus to show her his real form. He did so and the fire of his divine radiance killed Semele. But Zeus saved her unborn baby by sewing it into his own thigh. Months later, Dionysus was born from Zeus' thigh. The god gave the baby Dionysus into the care of a group of **nymphs**. When Dionysus grew up, these nymphs became his female followers, and were called Maenads or Bacchae. They were known for their wild behaviour.

In some parts of Greece, women commemorated Dionysus in a midwinter, outdoor festival. The god was also the centre of the City **Dionysia,** a festival in Athens, where **drama** was dedicated to him.

Dionysus's own love was **Ariadne** and he remained loyal to her for ever. He was the only faithful lover among the Greek gods.

46

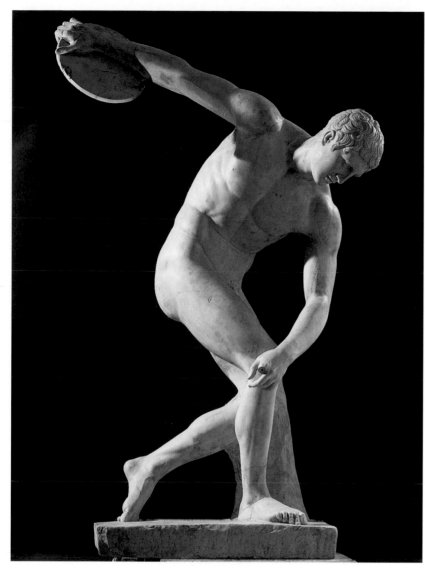

*A **discus** thrower. This is a Roman copy, in marble, of a Greek bronze statue.*

Discus

Throwing the discus was a popular sport. It featured in **athletics** competitions such as the **Olympic Games,** where it was one of the pentathlon events. Originally, Greek athletes used a large stone of suitable size and shape as a discus. Later, the athletes used a circular discus made of bronze. This weighed from 1.4 to 6.8 kilograms (3–15 pounds). By contrast, the modern discus weighs 2 kilograms ($4\frac{1}{2}$ pounds). It is possible that the heavier Greek ones were sometimes thrown underarm.

Drama

Greek drama developed from public performances of song and dance at religious **festivals** in honour of **Dionysus**. In very early times the performances consisted of songs based on myths, known as *dithyrambs*. It is thought that they were performed by a chorus, whose members may have danced as well as sung. Some time later, the tradition developed of an individual stepping out from the chorus and taking on the role of a character in the story. This development is associated with a poet called Thespis in the 6th century BC. In modern times actors are still sometimes called 'Thespians'. It became traditional for actors to wear masks and special costumes.

At the **Dionysia** festival in Athens there were drama competitions. The plays performed over the years included tragedies by the famous writers **Aeschylus**, **Sophocles** and **Euripides**. Some of these plays have survived, as

*This bronze **discus** is inscribed with the name of its thrower, Exoidas, and dedicated to Castor and Pollux, the twin sons of **Zeus**. Castor was known as a powerful discus thrower.*

47

Left: actors, wearing masks, in a modern production of an ancient Greek **drama**.

well as a number of comedies by **Aristophanes**.

Tragedies were usually based on myths and legends, but comedies were about contemporary life. There was wide freedom of expression as to what could be dramatized in a comedy. Male characters figure very prominently in Greek drama and all the actors were **men**. It is not known for certain whether **women** were allowed to go and see plays in the **theatre**.

Left: a small marble figure of an actor. His mask and costume show that he is playing the character of a slave. He is sitting on an altar.

Right: this vase shows two actors on stage. We know that this is a comic **drama** because of the types of masks and special padded costumes the actors are wearing

Education

A young person's education depended on several factors, including whether the child was a boy or a girl and which part of the Greek world he or she came from.

In **Athens**, education was the responsibility of parents because there were no state schools. Athenian men were expected to be literate in order to carry out their duties as **citizens**. Between the ages of six and fourteen, boys in Athens were taught to read and write, to memorize the works of **Homer** and to play the lyre and sing. Physical education took place at the **gymnasium**.

In **Sparta**, boys left home around the age of seven. They lived in state boarding schools where training to become soldiers was more important than learning to read or write. Spartan girls also went to school. It is not known how similar their education was to that received by Spartan boys, but they were treated more equally than in Athens, where educating girls was thought to be unnecessary.

*Musical **education**. A man teaches a young boy to play the lyre.*

Egypt

The civilization of Egypt (see map, page 5) flourished nearly two thousand years before the rise of Greece. Egyptian culture had a significant influence on Greek culture, especially in **sculpture** and technology. Before 1200 BC, **Mycenae**

probably traded with Egypt but there followed centuries of isolation when Egypt banned Greek merchants.

Eventually, around 650 BC, a Greek trading post was established at Naukratis on the Nile. Greek merchant ships sailed there, trading silver and slaves for much-needed grain. Egyptian luxury products such as carved ivory were also traded, but Naukratis fell into decline after **Persia**

took control of Egypt around 525 BC. Egypt remained part of the Persian Empire until it was conquered by **Alexander the Great**.

Alexander founded the famous city of Alexandria. After Alexander's death, one of his generals, Ptolemy, became ruler of Egypt. Ptolemy's descendants (including the famous Cleopatra) ruled Egypt from Alexandria until 30 BC.

*These figures of a lion and a bull come from Naukratis in **Egypt**. The bronze bull is the Apis bull, sacred to the Egyptian god Amun, but the writing on the base is in Greek.*

*The temple of the god Horus at Edfu in **Egypt**. The temple was built during the Ptolemaic period - the years when Ptolemy and his descendants ruled Egypt.*

Electra (Elektra)

In myth, Electra was the daughter of **Agamemnon** and Clytemnestra. She helped her brother Orestes to murder their mother in revenge for Clytemnestra's slaying of Agamemnon.

In the **theatre** many playwrights became interested in Electra's story because of the decisive role she took in making the revenge killing possible. Clytemnestra planned to murder the infant Orestes to prevent him seeking revenge when he grew up. Electra rescued Orestes and smuggled him out of the city. Years later, when Orestes returned to **Mycenae**, Electra recognized him at the tomb of their father and together they plotted to kill their mother. **Sophocles** wrote a play about Electra. In another version of the story, by **Euripides**, she dominates her brother, driving him to murder and helping to plunge a sword into Clytemnestra.

Eleusinian Mysteries

Eleusis lies about 24 kilometres (15 miles) outside the city of Athens (see map, page 62). It was home to a shrine to **Demeter**, the goddess of agriculture. Every year pilgrims came from across the Greek world to visit the shrine and participate in a secret religious cult. This cult became known as the Eleusinian Mysteries. Men and women, slaves and non-citizens all took part. The shrine held the largest roofed public building of its time. The exact nature of the ceremonies held there remained the secret of the cult's followers.

We know that participants walked in procession from Athens to Eleusis, copying Demeter's search for her daughter Persephone, and fasted as they did so. When they arrived at Eleusis they drank a special barley drink, in memory of

the kindness of a local woman who caused the goddess to smile and take a drink. Participants in the Mysteries believed that their devotion assured them a happier existence in the afterlife.

*A statue of Demeter, the goddess worshipped in the **Eleusinian Mysteries**. Demeter was also worshipped at a women's festival, the **Thesmophoria**.*

Elgin Marbles

Thomas Bruce (1766–1841) was the seventh Earl of Elgin. While serving as a British diplomat he became interested in the carved decorations of the **Parthenon** in Athens. After negotiating with the Turkish authorities who controlled Athens at the time, he was given permission to remove the sculptures, which he did in 1801. He shipped the marble sculptures back to England, where they became known as the Elgin Marbles.

In 1816 the sculptures were bought by the British Museum, where they are still on display. The poet Byron and others called Elgin a vandal for taking them. This is still a matter of controversy to this day. The Museum has protected and preserved the sculptures but the Greeks want them back. They belong in Athens, they say, and can be safely looked after there.

*Part of the **Elgin Marbles**. This section of the Parthenon frieze shows young citizens of military age riding in a procession in Athens.*

Elysium

Elysium was the home of the blessed in the Under-world. The Greeks believed the afterlife was dull and dreary for most people, but a few were singled out by the gods for eternal happiness in the Elysian Fields.

Endymion

Endymion was a shepherd and a son of **Zeus**. Selene, the goddess who carried the moon across the sky in her chariot every night, fell in love with Endymion. Selene persuaded Zeus to grant Endymion one wish. He chose eternal sleep while remaining young forever.

In another version of the myth, Selene sent him to sleep because she could not bear the thought of him losing his youth and beauty. Endymion and Selene had many children and lived either in southern Greece or in **Caria**.

Epicurus (Epikouros)

Epicurus founded a school of **philosophy** in a garden in **Athens** around 300 BC. His followers, who included women and slaves, became known as 'Epicureans'.

The principle of Epicureanism, written above the entrance to their school, was 'Pleasure is the highest good.' The Epicureans taught that the secret to a happy life lay in choosing a simple life with simple pleasures. Epicureans thought that wanting something you could not have caused pain and so they avoided desire for those things.

They thought that there was no afterlife: that the body and soul both disintegrated after death. They also believed that the gods do not interfere with our lives. This upset the many people who believed all the stories about the gods. Nevertheless, Epicureanism remained popular and was famous for the great friendship that existed among its followers. Some Romans adopted Epicureanism. The enemies of Epicureanism wrongly accused its followers of self-indulgence.

A marble bust of **Epicurus***, who lived from around 341 BC to 270 BC. He wrote many books about his philosophy but most of them are lost. We know about his teachings mostly from a Roman poet, Lucretius.*

Below: the **Erechtheum** *at* **Athens***. The caryatid porch can be seen on the left. Lord Elgin took one of the caryatids to London. The rest of the original caryatids have now been removed to an indoor museum to protect them from damage caused by air pollution.*

Erechtheum

The Erechtheum, a building on the **Acropolis**, dates from the 5th century BC. It is named after a mythical king of Athens, Erechtheus. The building is located just to the north of the **Parthenon**. The ancient olive-wood statue of Athena was kept there.

Records have survived showing how **slaves**, **citizens** and non-citizens were paid the same wage while working on the building. The best-known feature of the Erechtheum are the statues of clothed women, known as caryatids, that act as columns supporting one porch of the temple.

Eros

Eros, the Greek god of love, is often depicted as a child, sometimes with wings. He often carries a bow and arrow. Eros was thought to stir up feelings of love in the hearts of humans by shooting arrows at them. He had a mischievous personality. He was adopted by the Romans who gave him the name Cupid.

Eros was the son of **Aphrodite**. He fell in love with a princess, Psyche, whose name means Soul. He enticed her from her home to a magic palace in a distant land. Eros decided that they should only love in darkness and Psyche should never see what he looked like. Eventually Psyche decided she must see him, so she lit a lamp, but she dripped hot oil on his shoulder as he slept beside her. Eros fled with the cry that love cannot tolerate suspicion. After fulfilling difficult tasks set by Aphrodite, Psyche was finally reunited with Eros and they married.

Euripides

Euripides (485–406 BC) was the youngest of the three great dramatists that dominated the Athenian **theatre** with

*This 19th-century painting by Edward Burne-Jones shows winged **Eros** gazing on his sleeping lover Psyche.*

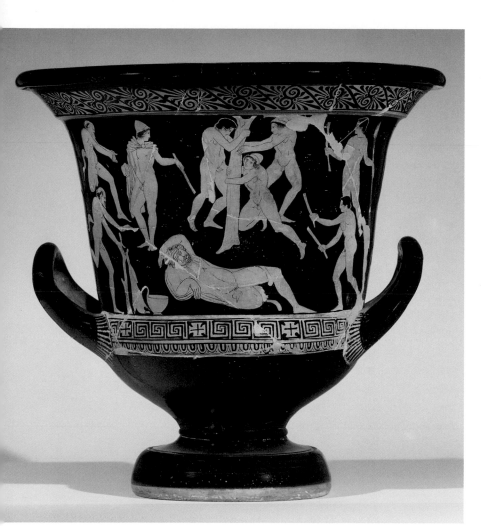

The two **satyrs** standing at the left of this picture of **Odysseus** and the Cyclops suggest that this is a picture of a play, perhaps by **Euripides**.

their tragedies. **Aeschylus** and **Sophocles** were the other two. Euripides gained a reputation in his own lifetime for his highly individual **dramas**. His play *Medea* is interesting for its strong female leading role. His *Trojan Women* is about the horror of war and how it affects the lives of women.

Euripides was the first person known to have owned a library. He was a friend of **Socrates** and knew the works of the Sophists. His plays won first prize at the **Dionysia** four times, which is few compared to Aeschylus, who won thirteen times, and Sophocles, who won eighteen times. However, nearly twenty of Euripides' plays have survived, which is more than twice as many of those of the other two dramatists. His daring treatment of the myths gave offence to many citizens.

Eurydice (Euridike)

Eurydice was the wife of **Orpheus**, an excellent lyre player. One day she was walking with her friends through a field in **Thrace** when she received a fatal bite from a snake. Orpheus was so upset at her death that he went to the Underworld to try to bring her back.

Orpheus played his lyre to the god **Hades** and his music was so lovely that he won the god's permission to take Eurydice back to the land of the living. However, Hades made one condition. He said that while they travelled, Eurydice must walk behind Orpheus and he must not look back at her until they had both reached the light of day.

Following behind her husband, Eurydice was able to leave the Underworld. But, just as they were about to reach safety, Orpheus felt a moment of anxiety. He glanced behind him and immediately Eurydice was dragged back into the dark below.

Exile

Exile, the expulsion of someone from his own **city-state**, was a common punishment in the Greek world. Wrongdoers were not usually put in prison, so exile was an effective way of dealing with individuals who were no longer welcome in their community.

The historian **Thucydides**, who was a general in 424 BC, failed to prevent the **Spartans** from capturing an important town during the **Peloponnesian War**. He was tried and exiled. In **Athens**, the system of **ostracism** was developed as a formal way of exiling undesirable citizens. Exile was sometimes the only way to avoid death: **Orestes** was sent into exile as a child to protect him. **Herodotus** chose exile to avoid a punishment after finding himself on the losing side in a political struggle.

Farming

The daily lives of the vast majority of ancient Greeks were based on farming and the production of essential food. Ploughing and sowing began in October, harvesting wheat and barley started in May, and winnowing the grain began in July.

It was not an easy life. People had only simple tools and the hilly terrain could make farming difficult (see **geography of Greece**). There was always the risk of a drought, which meant that the crops failed and people went hungry. Wherever the soil was rich enough to support crops, it was used for barley, wheat, **olive** trees, and grapes for wine-making. Poorer soils were used for grazing animals. Greek farmers grew figs, apples and pears. Beans were also grown, as well as flax, which was woven into linen. Any surplus in olives or wine could be sold for cash at the local market.

The average size of an Athenian farm was between 4 and 8 hectares (10–20 acres). A plough with a metal tip and a sickle for reaping were the essential tools. Most farmers who could afford them had **slaves** to work on the land. Sheep and other animals were kept for their milk, their hides and their wool rather than for meat. Oxen were the main working animals of Greek farmers. Horses were kept only by rich families for battle and travel.

Every farmer in **Athens** had certain rights. He could speak and vote in the **Assembly**. He could serve on a jury or even become a member of the Council, or a government official. Farmers also provided the hoplites, the soldiers of the city's armed infantry.

Olive groves at the foot of Mount Parnassus today. They would have looked very much the same at the time of the ancient Greeks.

*Right: a **farming** scene. This pot shows farm-workers shaking olives off a tree during the olive harvest. Two of them are wearing caps of leather or felt.*

Fate

The Greeks believed that Fate controlled human affairs and even controlled the gods. Mighty **Zeus** himself could not interfere with Fate. Homer's poem the **Iliad** sometimes describes Zeus holding a pair of scales, representing Fate, while two warriors fight. The idea is that, although Zeus is weighing the fates, he cannot affect the outcome of the fight, which is decided by Fate. It was Fate that presented **Achilles** with a choice between staying at home and living a long life, or going to **Troy** and dying young with fame and honour in battle. He chose to go to Troy.

The Greek word for fate was *moira*. The Moirai, the Fates, were three goddesses responsible for the unavoidable operation of fate. They are pictured as spinners and the thread they spin represents the fate of each individual human.

Festivals

Festivals included song and dance, a procession to the temple and a sacrifice to the god or goddess being worshipped. Festivals were religious events but they were also fun. People could go out of their homes, see their neighbours and enjoy what was taking place. Athletic and musical **competitions**, as well as competitions featuring **drama**, could be part of important festivals like the **Dionysia** and the **Panathenaea**.

In Athens, there were festival events of one kind or other happening on about half of the days of the year. They were not all equally important but there were more than thirty very important ones and many lasted for a number of days. Some of the Athenian festivals, such as the **Thesmophoria**, were reserved for women citizens. In other festivals, non-citizens, even **slaves**, had a part to play. There were also special roles for young people during some festivals.

*Women fetching water from a fountain-house. They may be preparing for a **festival**.*

Fish

Most ancient Greek people had a limited diet. They ate what they could grow or farm. Fish was one way of enlivening a meal with something tasty and different. Most people worked as farmers and did not have the means or the time to go fishing themselves. If they wanted fish they had to buy it. However, the Mediterranean is not especially rich in fish, so prices could be high and beyond the means of most families. Eating expensive fish dishes became a way of demonstrating wealth.

*The **fish** painted on this dish were all eaten by the Greeks: red mullet, bass, torpedo, sargus (not known today) and cuttlefish.*

Food

Most meals were based on cereals, mainly wheat and barley, with eggs, beans and other vegetables. The ancient Greeks ate bread with most meals. Meat was eaten only on special occasions such as at a **sacrifice**. **Fish** was fairly expensive and considered a luxury.

Carbohydrates in the diet came from bread and cakes. Legumes such as beans, lentils, and chick-peas provided protein, and fats came from the **olive** oil used in the cooking of food. Milk mostly came from goats and not cows. The Greeks used milk to make cheese, but not butter, and they did not drink much milk. There was no sugar, but honey was used as a sweetener and fruits like figs provided a sweet taste. Onions, garlic, lettuce, celery and cucumber were common vegetables, and fruits such as apples and pears were eaten. Lemons and oranges were not available. Grapes were mostly used for making **wine**.

All sorts of birds were eaten, not just ducks and geese but also swans, thrushes, pigeons, pelicans and nightingales.

Farming could be an unpredictable business, and most Greeks experienced food shortages at times. Only a tiny minority of rich people could afford not to work for their food. In Athens, during the **Classical Age**, over half of all the city's grain was imported from the Black Sea area. Breakfast for ordinary people might be no more than bread dipped in wine. The wealthy could afford to eat well and rich men indulged in a kind of drinking party known as a **symposium**.

Friendship

The Greeks thought of friendship as a relationship between people of roughly equal status who were able to help one another in some way. Friendship usually involved a sense of mutual obligation: if you helped a friend, then the friend should help you when the need arose.

*Bread was a staple **food** in ancient Greece. This is a terracotta figure of a woman making bread.*

The Greek word *xenoi* means strangers, people who are not fellow-**citizens**. Among the aristocratic class, there were rules about how to treat *xenoi*. They were offered facilities to bathe, a Greek custom after a journey, and a meal and lodging. In return, the stranger was expected to offer the same hospitality.

Funerals

Most ancient Greek people were buried, not cremated, when they died. The body was washed and dressed by **women**. Sometimes a coin was placed in the dead person's mouth. The coin was to pay **Charon**, the mythical boatman who ferried the dead across the river Styx into the Underworld. A small cake might be also left for Hades' dog, Cerberus.

The dead person's family kept the body at home for a period of mourning. Then the body was carried on a stretcher to the burial place. The family sometimes left food and drink at the graveside, for the benefit of the dead on their journey to the Underworld. During the **Classical Age** it was not common to bury objects like jewellery or weapons in a person's grave, though this was done in earlier times. If the family could afford the cost, the body was buried in a coffin made of wood or possibly even stone. Better-off

*A **funeral**: mourners at the laying-out of a dead person. This pot in the geometric style was made in Athens in about 700 BC.*

families would also pay for a marble gravestone, known as a *stele*, to be carved with a portrait of the deceased. Small personal items were often buried with the dead. At public funerals, after a battle in war, a public speech could be delivered.

A famous funeral speech in wartime was given by **Pericles**.

If a dead person was not buried, their spirit could not pass through the gates of **Hades**. The thought of remaining unburied was horrible to the Greeks. In a tragic **drama** by **Sophocles**, the tyrant Creon orders that the body of a young man called Polynices should be left unburied. The young man's sister, Antigone, defies Creon and buries him, and Creon condemns her to death.

Furniture

Most furniture consisted of chairs, stools, couches, tables and chests and was made of wood. The *klismos* was a chair with a curving back, and a seat of interlaced thongs where a cushion could be placed. A couch served not only as a bed but also as a place to recline during mealtimes, when a small table supporting dishes of food could be drawn up to it. There were no cupboards or wardrobes. Chests were used for storage, and cups and jugs could be hung on pegs from the walls.

This detail from a pot shows a servant carrying a stool.

*This marble gravestone shows a man sitting on a klismos, a chair without arms. Most Greek **furniture** was made of wood and has not survived, except in art.*

Geography of Greece

Communication and transport were difficult across the mountainous terrain of Greece. Roads were bad and there were few wheeled vehicles. Transport by sea around the **Mediterranean** was easier. When goods were transported across land it was usually in panniers, carried by men or mules. Communication between cities took place through envoys who travelled by road or by sea. The Greek terrain influenced the kind of **farming** and **warfare** that took place. It also led to the development of separate population centres – **city-states** – with their own laws, dialects and customs.

Geometric style

A style of **pottery** that emerged in Greece around the 8th century BC. The pots are painted with geometric patterns of lines.

Gods

The deities of the Greek **religion,** many of whom lived on Mount **Olympus**.

Gorgons

The Gorgons were female monsters. The most famous of the Gorgons was the snake-haired **Medusa**, who was killed by the hero **Perseus**.

*The mountainous **geography** of southern Greece made land transport difficult, and the ancient Greeks often preferred **seafaring** as a means of long-distance travel.*

Government

The forms of government in ancient Greece varied from place to place and from one age to another. Essentially, there were four main types: kingdoms, where power rested with a royal family; **oligarchies**, where a few families kept power; **tyrannies**, ruled by a tyrant; and **democracies**, where government rested with the citizens.

In the **Classical Age**, there was generally a shared sense that people lived under a set of laws even if the government was in the hands of a small group of rulers. However, in Sicily and parts of northern Greece, kings still ruled without being accountable to the people they governed. **Sparta** was also different from most other **city-states** in having two kings who inherited their power from two royal families, and were controlled closely by elected leaders, the ephors.

Greece

Modern countries mostly have clearly defined borders, with a capital city, but ancient Greece was not like this. There was no capital and no single government. Greece consisted of a number of small states, all independent, but linked by the Greek language and Greek culture. **Thrace**, part of which is now in modern Greece, was not Greek, and **Macedon** was regarded as a backward, distant part of the Greek world. The establishment of **colonies** extended the Greek world well beyond the land mass and islands of

The coastline of **Greece** is very jagged and indented. The Peloponnese is almost an island except for the narrow isthmus of Corinth with the sea on either side. The mountains in the north are difficult to cross, and acted as a natural boundary. Good farming land was in short supply and many groups of Greeks set off to the coast of **Asia Minor** to establish **colonies**. Nowhere in Greece is far from the sea, but Greek ships (see **seafaring**) avoided sailing across the open sea if they could and stayed near the coast.

The east and the south of Greece became more important than the west and north. Places like **Thessaly** tended to be isolated while **Macedon** remained separate for a long time. The narrow mountain pass at **Thermopylae**, in southern Thessaly, had to be negotiated by any army wishing to invade Greece from the north.

Black Sea

Adriatic Sea

THRACE

MACEDON

ITALY

THESSALY

Aegean Sea

Ionian Sea

ASIA MINOR

N

PELOPONNESE

Mediterranean Sea

100 m

100 km

CRETE

CYPRUS

THRACE

MACEDONIA

EPIRUS

Dodona

THESSALY

Mount
Olympus

Hellespont

Troy

LEMNOS

Aegean Sea

LESBOS

SKYROS

AEOLIS

PHRYGIA

ITHACA

Delphi
BOEOTIA
Thebes
Plataea
Aulis

Gulf of Corinth

Marathon

PELOPONNESE

Eleusis
Corinth
Mycenae
Athens
SALAMIS
ATTICA

CHIOS

Sardis

LYDIA

Olympia

Mantinea
ARCADIA
Argos
Epidaurus
Tiryns

SAMOS

Ephesus

IONIA

Miletus

CARIA

Bassae

MESSENIA

DELOS

SERIPHOS

NAXOS

Halicarnassus

COS

Ionian Sea

Pylos

Sparta

THERA

RHODES

LYCIA

N

Cretan Sea

100 m

100 km

Knossos

CRETE

A map of the mainland of
Greece and **Asia Minor**. For
a map of the whole Greek
world, see page 5.

modern Greece. The ancient Greek world
included parts of Libya and Cyprus, the
western coast of Turkey (see **Asia Minor**),
places around the Black Sea, Sicily and
southern Italy as well as settlements
along the east coast of the Adriatic Sea.
Mainland Greece has a wide peninsula in
the south known as the Peloponnese. It is
connected to central Greece by a narrow
isthmus at **Corinth**. Many important
events in Greece's history took place in
southern Greece and what is now Turkey.

Greeks

Ancient Greeks lived all around the
Mediterranean but believed they shared a
cultural identity as Greeks. They may
have lived under very different kinds of

government but they had a common
language and **religion**.

Four main ethnic groups made up
the people of **Greece**: the Dorians, the
Ionians, the Aeolians and the Arcadians.
Each of them lived in a different part of
the country and each spoke their own
dialect. The Dorians were invaders who
came into southern Greece after the fall
of the **Mycenaean civilization**. **Sparta**
became the best-known Dorian city. The
people pushed out by the Dorians – the
Ionian Greeks – moved across the sea to
a part of **Asia Minor** that became Ionia.
However, **Athens** and some parts of
central Greece were not conquered by
Dorians. A third ethnic group, the Aeolian
Greeks, inhabited **Thessaly** and parts of
Asia Minor. The Arcadians shared their
dialect with the people of Cyprus.

Gymnasium

The gymnasium (plural gymnasia) was an open-air sports ground. Gymnasia first appeared in the 6th century BC for the use of male citizens: men and boys. They played an important part in Greek life and **education** because of the importance of **athletics**.

As well as a running track and fields for throwing the discus and javelin, there would usually be a **wrestling** area, jumping pits and a changing area and bathrooms. Men trained in the nude. 'Gymnasium' comes from *gymnos*, the Greek word for naked. The athletes covered their bodies in oil and a fine dust. The gymnasium was a public area which also served as a social meeting place, especially for the aristocratic class, teachers and philosophers. Two of the most famous gymnasia in **Athens** were the Academy and the Lyceum, which became something like universities in the time of **Plato** and **Aristotle**.

*This is a model of the **gymnasium** at Olympia. It has a long practice running track which was roofed over so that the athletes could practise in rainy weather. There was space in the courtyard for discus and javelin practice. The gymnasium was swept away by a flood in the fourth century AD.*

H

Hades

Strictly speaking, Hades, a brother of **Zeus**, was the god of the dead. However, his name has also come to mean the Underworld, where humans dwelt after death (literally 'Hades' House').

The kingdom of Hades was not generally a place of punishment, although some wrongdoers, such as **Sisyphus**, and **Tantalus**, were punished there. But Greeks imagined it as a dreary and joyless place. The story of **Demeter and Persephone** is one of the few myths associated with Hades. Others involve **Heracles**, who wounded Hades when he tried to refuse him entry, and **Odysseus**, who also travelled to the Underworld.

When Hades was spoken of he was often referred to as 'Pluton', from the Greek word for wealthy, evoking the richness of the earth. When the Romans adapted Greek religion they called him Dis, meaning 'the rich'.

Sometimes heroes whom the gods liked went to the Isles of the Blessed, a place far away in the west of the world, where they lived a life of heavenly pleasure.

Hairstyles

Women liked to grow their hair long, though it was cut short at a time of mourning. Hair was fastened with a headband or gathered in a bunch or worn up on the head in a bun. Another style was to wrap the hair in a scarf and keep it

*This carved gemstone was made in the 16th century AD. It shows the punishment of a giant in Greek mythology, Tityus, who tried to rape the goddess Leto. His punishment was to have his liver eaten out by birds of prey in **Hades**, for all eternity.*

never went completely out of fashion. Slaves of both sexes kept their hair cut short.

Harpies

In myth, Harpies were winged females who would fly down to steal children. They appear in the legend of **Jason and the Argonauts.** Jason and his crew met Phineus, a blind king of **Thrace**, who was tormented by a curse. Every time Phineas tried to eat from a feast spread in front of him, Harpies came swooping down to snatch away his food. The Argonauts chased off the Harpies and rescued him.

*This figure is carved on a tomb from Asia Minor, usually called the 'Harpy Tomb'. She may be a Harpy or a **Siren**.*

*Examples of women's **hairstyles**. Women often bound up their long tresses with ribbon or with a hairnet.*

enclosed with the help of a pin, sometimes leaving a strand or two protruding from the scarf. Elaborate styles using curls and waves became fashionable only during the **Hellenistic Age**.

Men also grew their hair long, either tied with a headband or twisted into two plaits that could be wound around the head. Short hair became more common in the 5th century BC, as did a preference for shaving. However, growing a beard

Hector fights the Greek warrior **Achilles**.

Hector (Hektor)

In myth, Hector was a Trojan prince who led the defence of his city **Troy** against the Greeks. He died at the hands of **Achilles** in the tenth year of the war.

At Troy Hector conducted a daring and successful raid against the Greek ships. Achilles was refusing to fight at the time, but he permitted his friend Patroclus to take the field. Hector killed Patroclus, making Achilles so furious that he went back to the battle to seek revenge. Hector stood alone outside the gates of his city, while the king and queen of Troy urged their son to seek safety behind the city walls.

When Hector saw Achilles, he ran in fear from the man who **fate** had decreed would kill him. Achilles chased him three times around the walls until **Athena** tricked him by appearing in the form of his brother promising help. Hector decided to stand his ground, but when Athena disappeared he knew he had been deceived and he stood alone against Achilles. Hector fought bravely but the Greek warrior defeated and killed him.

Before the fight, Achilles rejected Hector's plea that the loser should have the right of a proper **funeral**. In his anger, Achilles tied Hector's dead body to his chariot and dragged it around Troy, before leaving the corpse for the dogs to eat. However, **Apollo** preserved the body and kept it from harm. The god **Zeus** and the pleading of Hector's father eventually

*This pot in the **geometric style**, from about 730 BC, shows a man and a woman beside a ship. They may be **Paris** and **Helen**.*

persuaded Achilles to relent and allow his enemy to be buried.

In the **Iliad**, Hector appears as a loving father and husband as well as a spirited and mighty warrior.

Helen

In myth, Helen was regarded as the most beautiful woman in the world. Helen was the daughter of **Zeus** and the Spartan queen Leda. She married Menelaus, the king of **Sparta**.

Helen ran away with **Paris** to **Troy**, so causing the **Trojan War**. After ten years of siege, the Greeks won the war and recaptured Helen. Menelaus at first intended to kill her, but he and all the other Greeks were won over by her beauty and forgave her. She returned to live with Menelaus in Sparta.

A 16th-century English playwright, Christopher Marlowe, described Helen as 'the face that launched a thousand ships, and burned the topless towers of Ilium'. (Ilium is another name for Troy.)

*This pot shows Menelaus angrily threatening **Helen** after the sack of **Troy**. The woman on the right may be the goddess **Aphrodite**, asking him to forgive Helen.*

Hellenistic Age

The Hellenistic Age refers to the history of the Greek world from the death of **Alexander the Great** in 323 BC until Rome conquered Greece in 30 BC. Rome was the heir of much Hellenistic culture.

The Hellenistic world stretched from southern France to the north of Afghanistan. Although Greece itself was still important, the cultural capital had shifted outside Greece to Alexandria in the north of **Egypt** and Pergamon in **Asia Minor**. An important library was established at Alexandria to preserve works of literature from **Homer** onwards.

The Hellenistic Age came to an end with the death of a famous queen in 30 BC. She was Cleopatra VII, the last Ptolemaic (that is, Greek) ruler of Egypt. She killed herself when **Rome** conquered her country.

*These terracotta figures made in the **Hellenistic Age** show women playing the game of knucklebones.*

Helots

The helots were the original people of Laconia. The **Spartans** enslaved them and made them work the land to provide their Spartan rulers with food. Helots also had to serve in the Spartan army. They were allowed to have families but were kept firmly under control and were treated brutally.

The Spartans officially declared war on the helots every year, fearing that they would rebel. A special secret police force was maintained to keep an eye on the helots. The conquered people of Messenia, a state neighbouring Laconia, were similarly subjected to serfdom. They revolted in 464 BC when an earthquake in Sparta caused turmoil and presented them with the opportunity. The revolt was put down.

In the **Peloponnesian War** helots fought on both sides. Messenia regained its independence in the early 4th century BC when Sparta was defeated by **Thebes**. The practice of subjecting and exploiting a class of serfs, or helots, was also found in other parts of Greece where Dorian Greeks like the Spartans lived.

Hephaestus (Hephaistos)

In myth, Hephaestus was a lame god, a blacksmith and the patron of craftsmen. He was the son of **Zeus** and **Hera**. After his parents quarrelled and Hephaestus took his mother's side, Zeus expelled him, hurling him off Mount **Olympus**. He landed on the island of Lemnos (see map, page 62), receiving an injury to his foot, which made him lame. However, he later returned to Olympus.

His wife was **Aphrodite**, and she was often unfaithful to him. Hephaestus constructed an ingenious metal net to catch her and Ares, the god of war, together. He then embarrassed them both by showing them to the other gods.

Hephaestus was often associated with fire. He was particularly celebrated on the volcanic island of Lemnos and in **Athens**.

Hera

The goddess Hera was one of the most important figures in Greek mythology. Many ancient **temples** across Greece were dedicated to the worship of this powerful goddess. She also became popular in **Rome**, where she was known as Juno. Various myths and rituals associate Hera with womanhood and marriage. Her husband was the mighty **Zeus** himself. It is possible that Hera's origins lay with an ancient, pre-Greek, worship of a powerful female spirit.

This is a section of the relief from the Parthenon, showing **Hera** and **Zeus** seated next to each other. Hera is drawing a veil over her face.

Heracles (Herakles)

The hero Heracles, known to the Romans as Hercules, was the son of the god **Zeus**. His mother, Alcmene, was a human. **Hera**, Zeus' wife, became angry that her husband had deceived her with another woman. She sent snakes to Heracles'

cradle to kill him and his half brother. Heracles strangled them. When Heracles grew up and married, Hera sent him into a state of madness and he unknowingly killed his wife and children. After seeking advice from the oracle at **Delphi**, Heracles went to work for King Eurystheus of Sparta for twelve years. The king gave Heracles twelve increasingly difficult labours to accomplish.

The first five labours involved killing or capturing dangerous beasts, such as the lion of Nemea and the hydra of Lerna, a great water snake. Heracles made a great club to tackle the lion, and the club became his favourite weapon. He accomplished the sixth task – cleaning the filthy stables belonging to King Augeas – by diverting the course of two rivers.

For his seventh labour he had to capture the bull of **Crete**, and, for his eighth, to capture the horses of a king of **Thrace**. Capturing the belt of the queen of the **Amazons** was the ninth task. The tenth task was to steal cattle from a monster in a faraway land.

The skin of the lion of Nemea could not be cut by any weapon, so **Heracles** had to strangle it to death. He skinned the animal using its own claws, the only way to pierce its skin, and wore the lion's skin as clothing.

The last two assignments were the most difficult: fetching Cerberus, the guard dog, from the Underworld (see **Hades**); and bringing back golden apples from the garden of the Hesperides. On his way to the Hesperides he freed **Prometheus**, and retrieved the apples with the help of **Atlas**. Heracles was finally cleansed of his crime.

Heracles accompanied **Jason and the Argonauts**, and he killed a **Centaur** who tried to harm Deianeira, his second wife. The dying Centaur tricked Deianeira. He told her that his blood was a love potion and would make Heracles love her forever. In fact it was deadly poison. She dipped a shirt in the blood and gave it to

Heracles is often shown in ancient sculpture as a figure of enormous strength battling with his enemies.

*Below: this woodcut by the German artist Albrecht Dürer shows **Heracles** and three unknown figures. Dürer lived in the fifteenth century AD; artists at this time were still familiar with the myth of Heracles.*

Heracles to wear. It stuck to his body and burned him terribly. So great was the pain that the hero threw himself onto a funeral pyre and died. Deianeira also killed herself when she realized what she had done. Heracles was made immortal and his spirit lived on Mount **Olympus**.

Heraclitus (Herakleitos)

Heraclitus is the best-known of the **Pre-Socratic** philosophers from **Ionia**, although not much of his writing has survived. Heraclitus did not look for fundamental substances that made up the world. Instead he found meaning in the unity of opposites: he pointed out that the path up a mountainside is also a path going down it.

'Everything is in flux', he said, and this continuous process of change applies to everything in the world, including ourselves. 'It is not possible to step into the same river twice' was one way he explained the nature of reality. He likened real things to a flame: it looks like a real object but it is really a *process* in the course of changing. Other sayings of his include, 'What anger wants, it buys at the price of the soul' and 'A connection that is hidden is stronger than one plainly seen'.

Hermes

Hermes was the messenger of the gods and a protector of travellers and shepherds. One of his tasks was to guide the dead to **Hades**, the Underworld.

Hermes was sent by his father, **Zeus**, to help **Odysseus** by ordering the nymph **Calypso** to release him from her island. He also gave Odysseus a magical plant to protect him from the magic of the witch **Circe**.

Greek people placed small wooden or stone statues of Hermes, known as herms, outside the gates of their houses. The god is sometimes shown carrying a magical wand and is associated with fertility. Hermes was a friendly and kindly god, with a love of mischief and a dislike of violence.

*Hermes is the messenger of the gods. He is often shown wearing sandals that speed him on his way and wearing or holding a sun hat. You can see him sitting on the left in this relief from the **Parthenon**.*

Herodotus (Herodotos)

Herodotus lived around 484–420 BC. He is famous as the world's first real historian. He was a Greek from **Caria**, in Asia Minor, at a time when Caria was controlled by **Persia**. As a child he may have watched the Carian fleet sailing out to join the Persian forces on their way to invade Greece. Later, Herodotus joined an uprising against his government and, when this failed, he went into **exile**.

He saw the struggle between Persia and Greece as a mighty conflict between two different cultures. He traced the development of the Persian Empire and events in Greece that led up to their conflict. The main topic of his book is the **Persian Wars**. Even though he saw the conflict as a struggle between freedom-loving Greeks and an unjust **tyranny** of the East, he tried to be fair to both sides. It was a great achievement to collect and organize information and present a history in this way. Although a Greek, Herodotus was not prejudiced against non-Greek societies and enjoyed writing about the customs of other cultures.

Hesiod

Hesiod, who lived around 700 BC, was one of the earliest Greek poets that we know about. He came from Boeotia (see map, page 73) on the Greek mainland.

The title of one of Hesiod's poems, *Theogony*, tells of the birth of the gods. The book describes how **Zeus** came to be the supreme god, and relates other myths that may have their origins in Asia. His other poem, *Works and Days*, is a useful source of information about social life and **farming** in early Greece.

Hesiod tells how he came from a place that was 'bad in winter, worse in summer, never good' and that he became a singer after meeting the Muses who breathed the gift of song into him.

Hippocrates (Hippokrates)

Hippocrates was the most famous physician and medical writer of ancient Greece. Hippocrates lived in the late 5th century BC and came from the island of Cos. He set up a school of **medicine** and established a system of medical practice that was based on observation, diagnosis and treatment, not on **magic**. A revised Hippocratic Oath, promising to care for the well-being of the patient, is taken by many newly-qualified doctors in America.

History of Greece

There were farming communities in mainland Greece (see map, page 73) at least as long ago as 6000 BC – some three thousand years before the **Bronze Age** began. A civilization first developed on the island of **Crete**, and later at **Mycenae** and other sites on the mainland.

Around 1250 BC there was a widespread breakdown of society in the eastern Mediterranean, though why this happened is not known. Archaeologists have confirmed the destruction of **Troy** and the abandonment of Mycenaean settlements. Shortly afterwards, people known as Dorians invaded southern Greece from the north. They settled in the Peloponnese, on Crete and in parts of **Asia Minor**.

There followed a period called the Dark Ages, because so little is known is about it. Then came a period of expansion known as the Archaic Age. Greeks began to settle in overseas **colonies**, cities such as **Athens** and **Corinth** began to develop, and the first **Olympic Games** took place in 776 BC. In some parts, political revolts broke out and rich aristocrats were forced to share power with people they once governed. The **city-state** of **Sparta**, however, stuck to its system of hereditary kingship.

In Asia Minor, a revolt by Greeks against the empire of **Persia** turned into a larger conflict when Athens sent assistance. The Persians invaded Greece and were defeated by the Athenians at the battle of **Marathon** in 490 BC. A second, much larger, Persian invasion took place ten years later. This time the Persians were defeated by the Greeks at the battles of **Salamis** and **Plataea**.

Most of the 5th and 4th centuries BC are known as the **Classical Age**. This was a period rich in art and culture. But it was also an age of conflict and **war**, which included a long struggle for power between Athens and Sparta. The origins of this war lay in the rise of Athens following the defeat of Persia. The Delian League, which was originally a defensive group of allies protecting themselves against invasion, was turned into the **Athenian Empire**. Fear of domination by Athens led to the **Peloponnesian War** between Athens and Sparta in 431–404 BC.

After the defeat of Athens, the reins of power and influence passed briefly to Sparta. In 386 BC Sparta made a treaty with Persia but this did not prevent ongoing conflicts between Greek states. **Thebes** became powerful and defeated Sparta in 371 BC at the Battle of Leuctra. Nine years later, at the Battle of Mantinea, a combined force of Spartans and Athenians defeated the Thebans.

In the 4th century BC, **Macedon** in northern Greece developed into a powerful state under King Philip and his son, **Alexander the Great**. After Alexander's death in 323 BC, the period known as the **Hellenistic Age** began.

After the Roman conquest of Greece in the second century BC, the states of Greece lost their independence.

The **history of Greece** included the development of Greek **colonies** around the Mediterranean and many wars between the Greek **city-states** and their neighbours.

Homer

Homer was the name the ancient Greeks gave to the author of the **Iliad** and the **Odyssey**, but almost nothing is known about the poet. Tradition holds he was blind and came from **Ionia** in **Asia Minor**.

The poems were probably written down in the mid-8th century BC. However, before this there had been a story-telling tradition in which groups of public reciters, called rhapsodes, memorized poems telling of mythical events. Homer may have been one of these rhapsodes. Whether Homer was the author of both poems is uncertain, but the Greeks thought so and they had tremendous respect for him and his poetry.

Both poems are set in the world of the **Bronze Age** in the thirteenth century BC, a time when **Mycenae** was the most powerful city in Greece. Thus there is a gap of over 400 years between Homer's time and the earlier Bronze Age that is the setting for his poems. This suggests that the poet was drawing on stories that had long been told by rhapsodes.

In the **Hellenistic Age**, at Alexandria in **Egypt**, there was a great deal of research into Homer's poems, and an official version of the text was agreed.

No one knows when or where **Homer** *was born, but it is thought that he lived in the 8th century BC. This portrait bust of Homer was made centuries later.*

Houses

A typical ancient Greek house was planned around a courtyard, with rooms built around it. The kitchen would often be in the courtyard itself and there might be a well for water. Some homes had an upper storey on one side of the courtyard, but many houses had just one storey.

Walls were built of mud-bricks or stone and rubble. The roof was tiled or covered with brush. Rich people's houses might have a separate bathroom with a clay bath and a drain leading outside the house. However, there was usually no drainage or toilet, and chamber pots were used. The inside walls of homes were plastered and sometimes painted or had textiles hanging on them. Floors were of beaten earth.

Most homes had an inside room with a loom, where **women** wove cloth. Women were kept secluded and safe. Another room would be reserved for **men**. There was little **furniture**. Windows were few, and the rooms were lit by daylight

The vase shows a rhapsode.

from the courtyard or from burning **olive** oil in lamps.

There was no fossil oil or coal and natural resources were limited. Most items and utensils for the home were made of clay (see **pottery**) or wood. As forests were cleared and wood became scarcer, Athenians would take the foundation timbers of their houses with them if they had to flee in time of **war**.

Hubris

Hubris is a Greek idea and there is no exact word for it in English. It means an act of excessive pride that leads to disaster. The Greeks believed that **fate** and the gods controlled their lives. People who became too ambitious were defying the gods and risked bringing the gods' wrath on themselves.

Herodotus, the historian, thought that the Persians were defeated because they showed too much pride in their empire and attempted to conquer the world. His story of **Croesus** concerns a man whose wealth and prestige led him to think too highly of himself. When Croesus thought he was about to die at the hands of the Persians, he called out the name of Solon. He remembered Solon's wise words that, while a man may

*An ancient Greek country **house** built around a courtyard. This drawing is based on modern excavations of a site south of Athens. The courtyard had a south-facing verandah which brought shade in the summer and protection from the cold winds in the winter.*

be very lucky in his life, he cannot be called truly happy until he has died. To take luck for granted is an act of hubris. The disaster that inevitably follows hubris is called **nemesis**.

Oedipus, **Tantalus** and **Xerxes** were among the many real and mythical characters whom the Greeks believed to be guilty of hubris and who paid the price.

Hunting

Hunting was both a sport and a way of obtaining meat for **food**. The Greeks used packs of dogs as well as bows and arrows, javelins and nets to hunt and trap wild animals such as deer and wild boar. Men also hunted hares, usually on foot, attempting to drive them into nets that had been prepared beforehand. Deer were sometimes first caught in traps and then killed with javelins. Rabbits, foxes and birds were also hunted.

*Home from **hunting** A bearded hunter, with his hunting dog, brings home a hare and a fox. Older men look on with satisfaction. This picture comes from a black-figure vase made in the 6th century BC.*

Iliad

The Iliad is a long poem, divided into twenty-four books. It mostly covers a few weeks during the ten years of fighting between the Greeks and the defenders of **Troy**. The author of the poem, **Homer**, fills in events from the past and tells the reader what will happen after the battle is over and the ten-year-long **Trojan War** has ended.

The poem is about the anger of the Greek warrior **Achilles**, who refuses to fight and so gives the Trojans the advantage. Finally, after the death of his friend Patroclus, Achilles returns to the battle and kills the Trojan prince **Hector**. After Hector's death and the Greeks' trick with the **Wooden Horse**, Troy falls.

Although much of the story is about honour and fighting, the Iliad also tells about the terrible price of war and how people cannot escape what **fate** has in store for them.

Ionia

Ionia (see map, page 23) was a region of **Asia Minor** settled by colonists from mainland Greece around the 11th and 10th centuries BC. The most important Ionian city was **Miletus**, which itself went on to establish its own **colonies** as far west as southern Italy. Ionia maintained close ties with **Athens** and played an important role in Greek culture and history. It was the birthplace of a new way of thinking, which questioned traditional

*The walls at Troy. According to Homer's **Iliad**, the parents of the Trojan warrior **Hector** stood on the city walls and pleaded with their son not to fight with the Greek **Achilles**.*

explanations of the world in terms of religion and myth. In the 6th century BC, a famous group of philosophers known as the **Pre-Socratics** came from Ionia.

Ionia was conquered by neighbouring **Lydia** and then became part of the empire of **Persia** when the kingdom of Lydia was conquered by the Persians. In 499 BC the Ionian Greeks rebelled against Persian rule. Athens sent warships to help and the rebellion spread to other parts of Asia Minor. It took the Persians five years to crush the rebellion. To prevent another revolt, Persia decided to attack mainland Greece. This led to two great invasions of mainland Greece by the Persians, as recorded by the historian **Herodotus**.

After the Greeks defeated the Persians the cities of Ionia looked to Athens for protection and together they formed a defensive alliance. This eventually turned into the **Athenian Empire** from which many Ionian cities revolted and joined **Sparta**. Sparta then made a deal with the Persians and handed Ionia back to them. It was not until the time of **Alexander the Great** that the Ionian cities regained their independence.

Ionic

A style of Greek **architecture**, characterized by slender, elegant columns and capitals decorated by scrolls.

Iphigenia

In myth, Iphigenia was the daughter of **Agamemnon** and Clytemnestra. When Agamemnon was about to lead the Greek army to **Troy**, the fleet was delayed by unhelpful winds at Aulis (see map, page 62). The goddess **Artemis** sent the winds. Agamemnon was told that he had to sacrifice his daughter to Artemis to persuade the goddess to change the winds. Iphigenia, tricked into believing

she was about to wed **Achilles**, was killed by her father. After Iphigenia's brutal death, her mother Clytemnestra turned against Agamemnon and murdered him when he returned in triumph from Troy.

In another, happier version of the myth, Iphigenia was saved by Artemis at the last moment and carried to safety in the land of the Tauri. There her duty was to prepare for sacrifice any shipwrecked strangers. One day she recognized two strangers as her brother **Orestes** and his companion Pylades. They took Iphigenia back to Greece.

*This pot shows **Iphigenia** about to be sacrificed. There is a deer behind her. In one version of the story **Artemis** saved Iphigenia and substituted a deer at the altar.*

Italy

From around 750 BC the Italian peninsula and **Sicily** became home to a number of Greek **colonies**. Settlers were attracted by the rich farmland and the possibility of trade with Etruscans. The Etruscans developed an advanced civilization in Italy before the rise of **Rome**.

The Etruscans traded with the Greek colonists and were influenced and stimulated by Greek culture. The Greeks gave the name 'Italia' to the south coast of the peninsula. After the conquest of Greece by Rome, the name Italia passed into the Latin language and became the name for the whole peninsula.

*A woman called Seianti, from the Etruscan civilization of **Italy**. The picture below shows her sarcophagus (coffin). Scientists have reconstructed Seianti's face (on the left) from her actual skull. The resemblance to the face on the sarcophagus suggests that the artist made an attempt to capture her likeness in clay. However, on the terracotta sarcophagus she looks much younger than she actually was when she died.*

J

Jason and the Argonauts

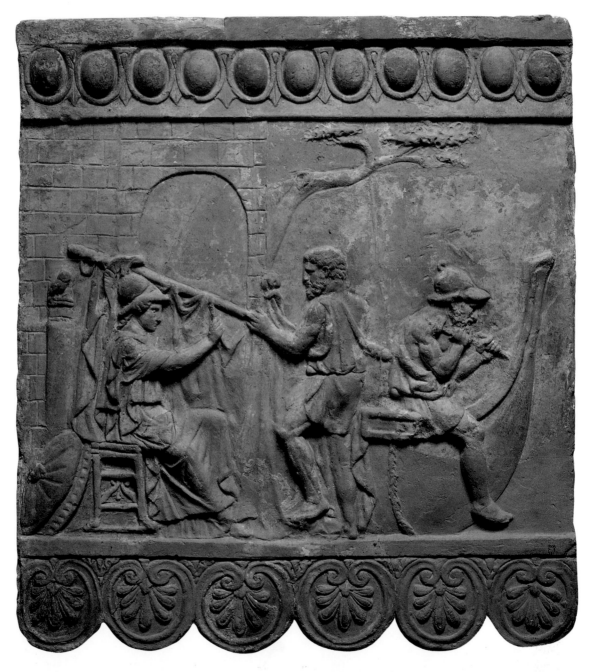

In myth, Jason was a prince from **Thessaly** who led the Argonauts – the sailors of the ship *Argo* – to the faraway land of Colchis (see map, page 5) in search of the Golden Fleece.

When Jason was a child his uncle Pelias seized his father's throne. Before Pelias could kill the child Jason, friends smuggled him out of Thessaly. Pelias had been warned to beware of a stranger coming to the kingdom with only one sandal. Years later, when the young Jason turned up, he had lost a sandal crossing a river on his journey. The worried Pelias persuaded Jason to leave on what he thought would be a hopeless mission, to find the fleece of a famed golden ram.

The Argonauts included the musician

*This terracotta plaque shows two craftsmen busy at work on the Argo, with the goddess **Athena** supervising. A shipwright named Argos built the ship and he accompanied **Jason and the Argonauts** on their adventure.*

Orpheus, the Spartan twins Castor and Polydeuces and the great **Heracles**. Their many adventures along the way included rescuing blind King Phineus from the terrible monsters the **Harpies**. Phineus was so grateful that he advised Jason on how to navigate through the dangerous Clashing Rocks. (This probably represented their journey through the narrow Bosporus into the Black Sea.) When they reached Colchis, Jason asked the king, Aeëtes, for the fleece. To earn it, he was given the seemingly impossible task of ploughing a field with dragon's teeth and killing the armed men that arose from the planted ground. Jason succeeded with the help of the king's daughter, the witch **Medea**, who gave him a magical potion. Later, Medea put a spell on the dragon who guarded the fleece and helped Jason to steal it.

An epic poem about Jason and the Argonauts, the *Argonautica*, has survived. It was written by a Greek poet and scholar, Apollonius of Rhodes. He lived in the 3rd century BC and was in charge of the famous library at Alexandria (see **Hellenistic Age**).

Jewellery

There were no zips or buttons, so men and women used pins and brooches to fasten their **clothes**. Women also wore jewellery for decoration including earrings, necklaces, bracelets and anklets. Bracelets were sometimes worn above the elbow as well as on the wrist. Men wore rings on their fingers. In **Sparta**, men's rings were always made of iron.

Ancient Greek jewellers produced very fine and detailed work despite having no means of magnification. By repeated hammering and heating, they produced metal sheets of gold and silver, and then shaped them with hammers and sometimes with moulds. Jewellers also made fine wire by hammering thin pieces of metal and rolling them repeatedly between sets of stones or metal plates. Metal punches were used to decorate the jewellery. Precious stones and glass were added for special effect.

*Items of **jewellery** were one of the few possessions that a woman could call her own. When she married she brought her jewellery with her to her husband's house and if they were divorced she would take her jewellery with her back to her parents' home.*

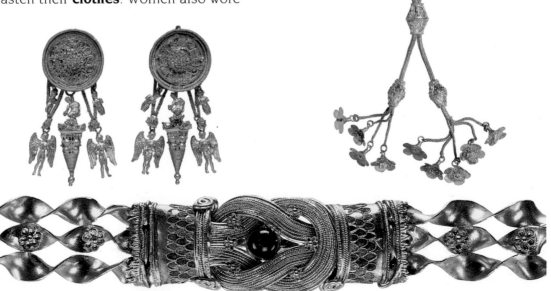

K

Knossos

The palace of Knossos was the centre of the **Minoan civilization**, which flourished in **Crete** from about 2000 to 1470 BC. The palace was discovered by the archaeologist Arthur Evans in 1900. Evans made many important discoveries, but he also set about reconstructing the palace, guided by how he imagined it looked. This is not how modern archaeologists work. The excavations at Knossos have revealed a sophisticated society that had the benefit of plumbing, including running water in clay pipes, a sewerage system and a flush toilet for the queen's dwelling area. Two- and three-storeyed buildings made up a complex of rooms and corridors, which probably gave rise to the myth of the labyrinth designed by **Daedalus** for King **Minos**.

*The remains of a royal room in the palace of **Knossos**. Excavations have continued, with only a few interruptions, since 1900 when Arthur Evans first discovered Knossos.*

*The north entrance to the palace of **Knossos** as Arthur Evans reconstructed it.*

Language

The Greek language was one of the foundation stones of Greek culture. As with English, there were many variations of the Greek language and people in different parts of the Greek world spoke their own dialects. However, the sense of sharing a common language was one of the main unifying factors among Greeks.

The earliest known form of Greek **writing** was first found on clay tablets at **Knossos**, and later at **Mycenae**. It was not until the 1950s that these were deciphered and shown to be an early form of Greek. The later Greek alphabet was adapted from the alphabet of **Phoenicia**. The main dialects of Greek – Doric, Ionic, Arcadian and Aeolic – corresponded to the main ethnic groups making up the Greek people.

LEARNING SOME GREEK

A	α	alpha	a
B	β	beta	b
Γ	γ	gamma	g
Δ	δ	delta	d
E	ε	epsilon	e (as in LET)
Z	ζ	zeta	zd
H	η	eta	e (as in WHERE)
Θ	θ	theta	th
I	ι	iota	i
K	κ	kappa	k, c
Λ	λ	lambda	l
M	μ	mu	m
N	ν	nu	n
Ξ	ξ	xi	x
O	o	omicron	o (as in GONE)
Π	π	pi	p
P	ρ	rho	r, rh
Σ	σ	sigma	s
T	τ	tau	t
Υ	υ	upsilon	y
Φ	φ	phi	ph
X	χ	chi	kh
Ψ	ψ	psi	ps
Ω	ω	omega	o (as in PORT)

This table shows the letters of the Greek alphabet, with their names, next to the equivalent English letters.

Try using the table to work out these three Greek words that have entered our language. (Answers below.)

    1. ασθμα   2. γραμμα   3. πλασμα

Now try to work out the English words that come from the following Greek words. (Answers below.)

    4. δραμα   5. αρωμα   6. προβλημα

ABC in Greek

Greek letters, as well as many Greek words, have become part of our language. Scientists have a tradition of using Greek letters and words to name new discoveries, which is why there are alpha, beta, and gamma particles (named after the first three letters of the Greek alphabet).

    The Greek letter pi (English p), π, has become an international symbol for mathematicians, representing the ratio between the circumference of a circle and its diameter.

    The mouth of a river that forms a triangular shape as it spreads itself out in different channels is called a delta after the Greek letter Δ.

1. asthma 2. grammar 3. plasma 4. drama 5. aroma 6. problem

The word inscribed on this lead sling shot, dexa, *means* **'take that'.**

This is part of an inscription from a temple in Asia Minor. It reads Basileus Alexandros *(King Alexander). The inscription goes on to say that the king has dedicated the temple to Athena.*

Law

Each **city-state** made its own laws. In the early days laws were made up by small groups of aristocrats and were unwritten. Later they were written down and displayed in public. At **Athens** the laws of the famous lawmaker **Solon** were first inscribed on wooden panels that were placed outdoors for all to see. These laws were later inscribed in stone for public viewing. Other cities displayed their laws in the same way. In a **democracy**, such as Athens, new laws could be proposed in the **Assembly**. **Sparta** had no written law code.

Law courts

Before the rise of **democracy**, justice was administered by aristocratic rulers or official magistrates. Trial by jury began in the 5th century BC in **Athens**. Only male **citizens** over the age of thirty could serve on a jury, which might consist of hundreds of, and sometimes over two thousand, jurors. They were chosen by lot and a payment was made to jurors to encourage their attendance.

Whatever the charge, the defendant and the accuser were each given the same amount of time to plead their case. A water **clock** measured out the time. Only a male relative of the victim could bring a case against someone for murder. There were no professional judges or lawyers, but speechwriters could be hired to compose effective speeches. **Women** could not be called as witnesses, and the evidence of **slaves** was admissible only if it had been obtained by torture. If a woman was accused of a crime, she could be represented by her husband or father.

Because of the size of the juries, there were no discussions and a vote took place immediately by placing small stones or discs into urns. Punishment took the form of fines, **exile**, loss of citizen rights and property, or death (see also **ostracism**). People were not imprisoned as a punishment.

Lesbos

Lesbos, a large island in the eastern Aegean Sea (see map, page 62), first became one of the **colonies** of Greece in the 10th century BC when Aeolian Greeks settled there. Kilns, for making the storage pots known as amphorae, have been found on Lesbos.

With the coast of **Asia Minor** only 10 kilometres (6 miles) away, Lesbos traded with non-Greek **Lydia** as well as **Egypt** and mainland Greece. The island's success was based on its overseas trade. After domination by **Persia**, Lesbos joined the Delian League and later revolted against the **Athenian Empire** that emerged from it. The female poet **Sappho** came from Lesbos.

Lydia

The kingdom of Lydia (see map, page 23) was a non-Greek state that dominated **Asia Minor** before it was conquered by **Persia** in the middle of the 6th century BC.

During the rule of King **Croesus**, Lydia, with its capital city Sardis, became famous for its wealth. Lydia had excellent trade routes to the east and west and had its own reserves of gold and silver. The world's first **coins** were minted in Lydia in the late 7th century BC. Under Persian rule, Lydia remained an important province until it was conquered by **Alexander the Great**.

M

Macedon

Macedon was a kingdom on the northern fringe of the Greek world (see map, page 62). Geographically, it was made up of a large plain surrounded by mountains. Macedon was conquered by the Persian king Darius and remained part of the Persian Empire until the defeat of **Xerxes** in 480 BC. Although the people of Macedon spoke a dialect of the Greek **language**, Macedon was not always regarded as fully Greek and it did not emerged as a powerful Greek state until the 4th century BC. Under King Philip and then his son **Alexander the Great**, Macedon conquered the whole of Greece and went on to add the Persian Empire to its own vast dominion.

*The reconstructed head of Philip II of **Macedon**. The reconstruction is based on a skull found in a tomb uncovered by archaeologists in the late 1970s. The remains in the tomb are thought to be those of Philip II. It is known that Philip was wounded in the face in a battle, and the skull had signs of a serious injury to the right eye socket.*

Maenads

Female followers of the god **Dionysus**. They were known for their wild, uncontrolled behaviour.

Magic

Evidence of magic in the everyday life of ancient Greece has been found in curses inscribed on thin sheets of lead. Many of

*This pot shows the sorceress **Medea** holding a spell-wheel which she used for her **magic**.*

these curse tablets express envy and hatred of someone for a personal reason and call for **revenge**. Charms and amulets were used to ward off evil, banish an illness, attract good luck or secure the affections of a loved person. Magic was a part of Greek **religion** and features in Greek myths concerning characters such as **Hermes** and **Orpheus**. Witches in mythology include **Circe** and

Medea. The **Thessaly** region was particularly associated with witches who could influence the moon. The goddess of witchcraft was Hecate.

Marathon

The Battle of Marathon in 490 BC was one of the most famous in ancient Greece. The battle was fought between **Athens** and the Persian army. **Persia** was seeking revenge against the Athenians for supporting their fellow-Greeks in Ionia who had rebelled against Persian rule.

Persia sent a fleet to Greece and landed an army east of Athens in the Bay of Marathon. The **Assembly** decided to send their army out to defend Athens, even though they were heavily outnumbered. A brilliant battle plan helped the Athenian leader Miltiades achieve a startling victory. One of the Athenians ran all the way to the city with the good news. The messenger died from exhaustion after saying to his fellow Athenians, 'Greetings, we win.' The legend of this messenger's journey lay behind the marathon race that was invented for the first modern **Olympic Games** in 1896.

The Battle of Marathon was enormously important to the Athenians. When, for example, the great playwright **Aeschylus** died, the words on his tomb made no mention of his poetry but simply stated that he had fought at Marathon. However, the Battle of Marathon was only the first chapter in a conflict between Greece and Persia, and the **Persian Wars** continued on a much larger scale.

Marriage

In **Athens**, and probably in other parts of Greece, girls married at around the age of thirteen or fourteen to men of about thirty. Most marriages were arranged by parents but there were also professional matchmakers. In **Sparta** both men and women may have married around the age of thirty and there was probably far more equality between them than in other **city-states**.

In Athens, where polygamy (having more than one wife) was not allowed, a

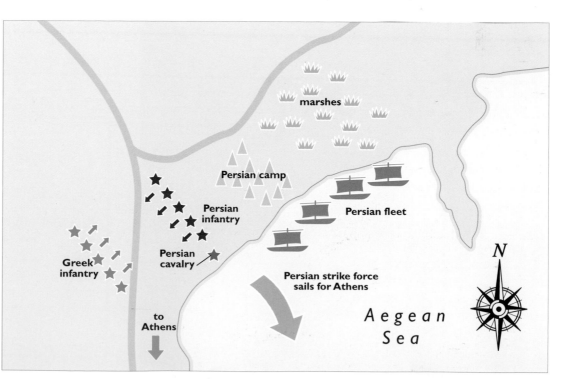

*The Battle of **Marathon**. The Athenians thinned out their line of soldiers to match the length of the larger Persian army but they reinforced each end, their wings. They charged on foot across the plain of Marathon towards the Persians, who broke through the centre of the Athenian line. But the Athenians were stronger at their wings and here they were able to break through the Persian line and wheel inwards to crush them. Over 6,000 Persians were killed. The 192 Athenians who died were regarded as great heroes. They were buried under a mound, which may still be seen at Marathon.*

marshes

Persian camp

Persian fleet

Persian infantry

Persian cavalry

Greek infantry

Persian strike force sails for Athens

to Athens

N

A e g e a n S e a

This scene wound its way around the outside of a jewellery or cosmetics box. It shows a **marriage** procession leaving for the bridegroom's house at night. The attendants sang a wedding song as the veiled bride journeyed to her new home.

marriage began with a public agreement with witnesses. The marriage ceremony began with the bride cutting her hair and having a ritual bath. This was followed by a wedding feast at her home, where she remained veiled and sat with other women. When night came she was brought, still veiled, in a marriage chariot to her new home. She was accompanied by a torchlight procession and the singing of wedding hymns. Her mother-in-law would be waiting to receive her. Both the bride and groom were showered with nuts and dried fruit, rather like confetti, before the bride ritually removed her veil.

Divorce was, in theory, a fairly straightforward matter, with either the husband or wife able to end a marriage.

However, in practice a woman needed the support of her father or brother to do this. When a well-to-do woman was divorced, or if her husband died and she was no longer welcome in the home, her dowry had to be returned and this would be used again if she remarried.

Mathematics

The origins of Greek mathematics are not clear, but it seems likely that the older civilizations of Mesopotamia and Egypt made important contributions. Pythagoras, who lived in the 6th century BC, is credited with a famous theorem that bears his name (see the diagram on

*Household items were carried in the **marriage** procession to the bridegroom's home.*

The Pythagoras theorem applies to any triangle with a right angle, that is, 90° (here represented by the square in the corner). Pythagoras proved that the square on the side opposite the right-angle (ABRS) occupies the same area as the squares on the other two sides (BFPC and ACQH) put together.

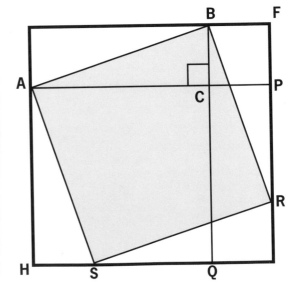

Geometry is Greek

The study of how patterns in space fit together is called geometry. The name comes from a Greek word geometria, meaning 'land survey'. When Pythagoras worked out his geometric theorem, he was so happy that he sacrificed a hundred oxen to the gods.

page 86). He is also associated with the important discovery that music and mathematics are related. Pythagoras showed, for example, that there is a 2:1 ratio between the length of strings and the octave sounded. You can hear this if you play a note on a stringed instrument and then, by holding a finger down on that string about half way along, play it again. You hear the same note, but one octave higher.

No writings by Pythagoras survive; nor do any by other famous mathematicians that came after him in the 5th and 4th centuries BC. Euclid, however, who was working in the **Hellenistic** city of Alexandria in **Egypt** around AD 300, wrote a textbook that has survived. Until only about a hundred years ago this book was used to teach mathematics in schools.

Medea (Medeia)

Medea was a woman who possessed powers of **magic**. She came from Colchis, to the east of the Black Sea, where her father was the king. **Jason and the Argonauts** came to Colchis to find the Golden Fleece and Medea fell in love with Jason. She used her magic to help him to steal the Golden Fleece.

According to the legend, Medea escaped with Jason to **Corinth**. Later, when there was a plan to banish her from Corinth so that Jason could marry someone else, Medea used her magic to kill the other woman.

Greek writers often presented Medea as a scheming witch and a barbarian. In a play by **Euripides** she murdered her own children rather than leave them with Jason and another woman.

*This picture on an Athenian vase from the 5th century BC depicts **Medea** as a witch who can use **magic** to restore youthful vigour to an old ram. In her left hand she holds the magic potion that is poured into the heated cauldron.*

Medicine

Before the time of **Hippocrates** and his followers, much of ancient Greek medicine relied on magical prayers, charms and the wearing of amulets. Special plants and herbs were thought to have healing powers. People made offerings to **Asclepius**, the god of healing.

The most important sanctuary dedicated to Asclepius was at Epidaurus (see map, page 62), where patients who came for a cure would spend a night in a special building, hoping to be visited by the god in their sleep. Archaeologists have found inscriptions at Epidaurus from grateful pilgrims recording their thanks to the god for their recovery.

Medicine adopted a rather different approach around the 5th century BC, when illness was thought to come from an imbalance of fluids, or humours, in the body. Doctors believed that at some stage in an illness the unhealthy fluid could be channelled through the blood. For this reason bloodletting was a standard treatment. Both the theory of humours and the practice of bloodletting became enormously influential over the next two thousand years.

*This marble stela carved with a leg has an inscription to **Asclepius**. It was probably given by a patient to thank the god for healing his leg injury. The Greek letters read: 'To Asclepius and health-bringing Fortune, a thank-offering'.*

Mediterranean

Few parts of the Greek world were very far from the Mediterranean Sea. As **Socrates** may have said, 'we live around the sea like frogs around a pond'. Even though **seafaring** was not an advanced art, journey by sea was the most common way of travelling a long distance and the numerous beaches and places to anchor encouraged sea travel.

When **Xenophon** and his army reached the end of their momentous journey from the heart of the Persian Empire, they knew they were safe when the sea came into view. *'Thalatta, thalatta!'* ('The sea, the sea!'), they cried. The Mediterranean helped define the world of the Greeks. It was the cradle of their civilization, which had its origins in the seafaring **Minoan civilization** and in myths of **Odysseus**, **Heracles** and **Jason**.

Medusa

Medusa was a female monster, the most important of the three dreaded Gorgons. Her hair was a mass of writhing snakes and her face so grotesque that anyone who caught sight of it was instantly turned to stone. Unlike her two sisters, Medusa was mortal. She was killed by

Perseus, who used his shining bronze shield as a mirror to avoid looking at her directly.

After Medusa's death, her children Chrysaor and **Pegasus** sprang forth from her decapitated body. Medusa's head retained its deadly power and Perseus kept it hidden in a bag until **Athena** took it to use against her enemies.

Men

Men took the leading role in Greek society. Only men engaged in warfare and politics, trade and farming. **Women** kept house, cared for children, and might support men's work, but they were expected to keep mostly out of view. In **Athens** boys from wealthy families received an **education**. Older boys, called *ephebes*, were given military training. Poorer boys would learn a craft or skill from their fathers. Unlike women, men had the chance to get together in public. Books written by **Plato** describe how groups of men met to have philosophical discussions. Comic plays (see **drama**) also show how life in Athens was dominated by men. One or two plays have strong female characters, but the actors who played the parts were all men. In Classical Athens men were either **citizens**, resident foreigners, or **slaves**. Only citizens – that is, sons of a citizen father and mother – could take part in politics. At the age of eighteen they could attend and vote in the **Assembly**, and at thirty could be selected for service on the Council. In wartime, men had to fight for their city. The richer men had to provide themselves with a horse and the equipment of a cavalryman. The less wealthy served in the infantry as **hoplites**, and the poorest rowed the warships.

Mercenaries

Mercenaries are men hired by a state to fight in battles. There were quite a lot of mercenaries in ancient Greece, because **war** was such a common feature of life. One of the earliest inscriptions in Greek to have survived is a graffito that a Greek mercenary from the 6th century BC scratched onto a huge statue at Abu Simbel in **Egypt**, 1,100 kilometres (700 miles) up the Nile.

The most famous Greek mercenary army was that of **Xenophon** and his

10,000 men, who fought in Persia and found their way back to Greece. Mercenaries were employed by both sides during the **Peloponnesian War**. There were specialist forces, such as archers from **Crete** and slingers from Rhodes who could sling a stone farther than an arrow shot from a bow and at 90 metres (100 yards) could inflict deadly wounds.

Metals

Bronze and, later, iron were made in ancient Greece, and important everyday objects such as weapons and plough-shares were made from them. Copper was imported from Cyprus, but the tin that was mixed with it to make bronze was in short supply. These metals had to be

*An example of the ancient Greeks' skill in working **metals**. This griffin head is hollow-cast from bronze. It was originally attached to a large bronze wine bowl. Perhaps the maker intended the griffin to guard the wine! It is beautifully made, showing all the details of the griffin's skin and features.*

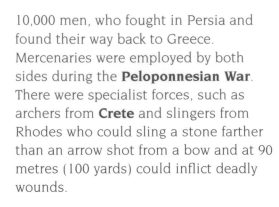

***Mercenaries** sometimes came from the non-Greek world. This soldier wears elaborately patterned clothing with long sleeves, unlike Greek soldiers.*

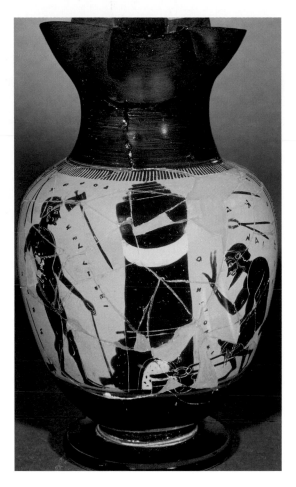

*Working with **metals**.*
A blacksmith tends his furnace
on this black-figure pot. Iron ore
was smelted in this kind of
shaft-furnace and then poured
into moulds to make ingots. The
ingots could then be taken to
where the iron was to be used.

extracted from ores by smelting, and the liquid metal was extracted. Metal objects made in this way were scarce and therefore valuable. The most valued metals were silver and gold.

The prosperity and success of **Athens** were partly based on wealth from the very rich silver mines discovered at Laurium, south-east of the city. As many as 30,000 workers, mostly slaves, dug and tunnelled for the silver at Laurium. The mines belonged to wealthy Athenians (see **Mining**).

There were also silver and gold mines in **Thrace**. In the 4th century BC, **Macedon** grew rich on its exploitation of gold mines at Mount Pangaeum.

Miletus

The Greek city of Miletus (see map, page 23) was the most important **city-state** in **Ionia**, on what is now the western coast of Turkey. It was first settled by Minoans and later by Greeks from **Mycenae**, before becoming an Ionian city around 1000 BC. Miletus was very successful as a trading centre between **Asia Minor** and mainland Greece, especially in wool, metals and olive oil. The city became so wealthy and big that it established its own colonies along the coast up to and including the Black Sea.

Miletus was at its height in the early 6th century BC. The city produced the world's first known philosophers and scientists, including **Thales** and **Anaximander**. The city's cultural independence came to an end after a revolt against the rule of **Persia** at the beginning of the 5th century. Following the eventual defeat of Persia, Miletus joined the Delian League and so became a member of the **Athenian Empire**. Towards the end of the **Peloponnesian War** Miletus, having supported Athens, changed sides and became an ally of **Sparta**, but Sparta returned it to Persian rule. Miletus regained its independence when **Alexander the Great** conquered Persia. However, Miletus lost its importance as a trading power as its harbour gradually silted up.

Mining

Mining for **metals**, both precious metals and metals for everyday use, was an important activity in ancient Greece.

The Greeks did not know how to locate particular metals (ores) in rock beneath the ground. They depended on finding an outcrop of a rock that they recognized above the surface of the earth. They then dug a pit to reach the ore and abandoned the mine when all the ore was gone.

If a vein of ore went deeper into the ground, Greek miners would dig vertical shafts to reach it. At Laurium, south-east of Athens, the deepest silver-mine shaft was 119 metres (390 feet) deep.

Minoan civilization

The Minoan civilization that flourished on the island of **Crete** (see also **Knossos**) was not Greek, but it had a major influence on later Bronze Age Greek communities in Crete and mainland Greece. Archaeologists named the civilization 'Minoan' after the legendary king of Crete, **Minos**.

Minoan civilization began sometime in the third millennium BC. It was based on trade with **Egypt** and with other lands around the **Mediterranean**. A number of Minoan families became prosperous and began building large palaces. The confidence of the age was shown by the fact that the Minoans felt no need to fortify their palaces against enemies. They decorated their rooms with pottery and with wall-paintings illustrating colourful scenes. Today, you can visit Knossos and see some of the palace rooms reconstructed by the famous archaeologist Arthur Evans.

The Minoans seem to have enjoyed watching a dangerous sport in which young men leapt and somersaulted over bulls. This probably accounts for the

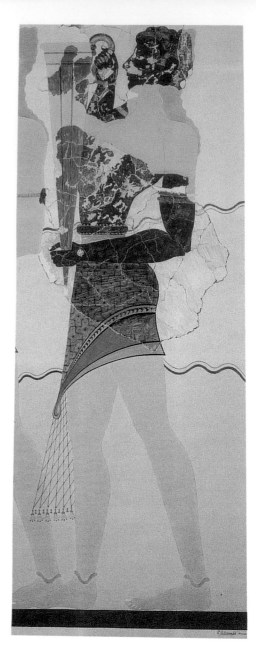

Above: a modern copy of a figure from a Minoan wall painting.

myth of King Minos, and also the story of **Theseus** and the Minotaur, a monster who was half-bull and half-man.

The Minoans were an advanced society – the first **Bronze Age** culture in the Mediterranean. The Minoan civilization collapsed around 1,470 BC, partly as a result of the rise of the Mycenaeans of Greece. But the legacy of the Minoans remained important to the development of Greek civilization.

Wall paintings with griffins in a room at the Minoan palace at **Knossos**. *The archaeologist Arthur Evans excavated and partly rebuilt the palace in the early twentieth century. He uncovered this room in 1900 and called it the 'throne room'.*

Minos

Minos was a legendary ruler of **Crete.** He established his right to the throne by asking **Poseidon** to bring a bull from the sea. Minos should then have sacrificed the bull to the god, but instead he kept it. Poseidon punished him by making the king's wife fall in love with the bull.

Daedalus was employed to design a device to bring them together, and the wife of Minos gave birth to a creature – half-bull, half-man – called the Minotaur. Daedalus was then ordered to design a maze to contain and hide the Minotaur. The creature lived in this labyrinth until the hero **Theseus** arrived. The daughter of Minos, **Ariadne**, helped Theseus find his way through the labyrinth and he killed the Minotaur.

Daedalus escaped with his son, Icarus, but Minos tracked them down to the island of **Sicily**. Minos was killed in his bath by a daughter of the king of Camicus in Sicily.

According to the myth of the Minotaur, it was the duty of **Athens** to send young people every year to Minos, to be offered to the Minotaur. This story probably dates back to a time when Crete was a formidable force, based on sea power, and less powerful **city-states** such as the early Athens had to send gifts to Crete to prevent war.

Money

Before the introduction of **coins**, Greek people traded by exchanging goods of equal value, or valuable objects such as silver, axes and the iron cooking spit called the *obolos*. This eventually gave its name to the smallest silver coin, the *obol*. There were six obols in one *drachma*. Half a drachma was barely a living wage for a day's work in the 5th century BC and a skilled craftsman would receive one drachma.

Records of the money spent on public projects, such as a temple, were carved on stone and displayed for all to see. From such accounts we know, for instance, that a large job like making the ornamental grooves – called fluting – along the length of a 6-metre (20-foot) column would cost 350 drachmas. Sometimes money could be kept in temples and the temple would also provide loans, but individual bankers also operated, making loans and exchanging currencies.

Muses

The nine Muses were the goddesses of poetry, dance and music. They were the daughters of **Zeus** and Mnemosyne, the goddess of memory. The Muses were

*This is a section of a marble relief carving showing the **Muses** with **Homer**.*

singers who dedicated their art to the gods and inspired humans in all forms of artistic communication, from poetry to speech-making. **Homer** begins his epic poem, the **Odyssey**, with a call to one of the Muses to help inspire him to tell the tale of Odysseus. **Hesiod** begins a poem by describing how, when he was a young shepherd on the mountainside, the Muses came to him with the gift of song.

The Muses were adopted by the Romans, who assigned separate skills to each one. The nine Muses were Calliope (epic poetry), Clio (history), Euterpe (flute-playing), Erato (lyric poetry), Melpomene (tragedy), Thalia (comedy), Terpsichore (dancing, lyric poetry), Polyhymnia (mime) and Urania (astronomy).

Music

Music was an important part of Greek life. It was closely associated with poetry and poetry-reading would be accompanied by music. That is how the Greeks would have experienced the poetry of **Homer**. Music was also a part of plays at the **theatre**, of public events like sacrifices and religious **festivals**, and of **funerals** and **marriages**.

This musician is holding a type of lyre. The pegs for tuning it can be seen on the cross-bar at the top. The first soundboxes were tortoise shells but these were improved on by making wooden boxes lined with ox hide.

Sparta was famous for its cultivation of music and its army marched into battle accompanied by music. Musical competitions were a feature of most games and of festivals such as the **Panathenaea**. Music and song also accompanied a private party like a **symposium**.

The two main musical instruments were the lyre, a seven-stringed instrument played with the hand, and a flute-like wind instrument called the *aulos*. There were also the pan-pipes, a set of up to seven pipes that were bound together and played through a mouthpiece. The importance that music held for the Greeks is reflected in the fact that the lyre

The man on this pot is holding a cithera, a larger version of the lyre.

was associated with the god **Apollo.** Also, music features in the **myths** of **Orpheus** and other heroes. Learning to play the lyre was a normal part of the **education** of a young man in **Athens**. Few fragments of musical scores have survived, but it would seem that music was all melody and no harmony.

Mycenae

The city of Mycenae (see map, page 62) was the centre of the **Mycenaean civilization**, which developed between around 1600 and 1200 BC. **Archaeology** directed by Heinrich Schliemann led to important discoveries at Mycenae in

Looking out through the Lion Gate at **Mycenae**.

1876. These included a number of rich tombs, one of which contained a gold death mask that Schliemann claimed belonged to **Agamemnon**, the leader of the Greek expedition to **Troy**. It is now known that Schliemann was wrong. The tombs really date from the 16th century BC, hundreds of years before any likely expedition by Greeks to Troy.

The city of Mycenae was surrounded by limestone walls with a monumental Lion Gate. This gate has a massive triangular slab above it with two sculpted lions either side of a column. Another giant lintel, above the door of the 'Treasury of Atreus' (in fact a beehive-shaped tomb), is formed of a single block of stone weighing 120 tonnes.

Mycenaean civilization

Even before the collapse of Minoan power in Crete around 1470 BC, **Mycenae** was the centre of the first Greek civilization to dominate the south Aegean and parts of **Asia Minor**. Other important Mycenaean settlements were Tiryns, Pylos and **Thebes**. The relationship between Mycenaean civilization and the **Minoan civilization** of **Crete** remains unclear. It is not known for sure how responsible the Mycenaeans were for the destruction of Minoan power. What is certain is that Mycenaean society, which flourished after the Minoan collapse, had been deeply influenced by the Minoans in writing, art and crafts and the practice of building large palaces for the rich, ruling families. A feature of Mycenaean society was the construction of chamber tombs carved into soft rock or built out of stone.

The power and wealth of Mycenaean society was based on trade. Mycenaean pottery has been found throughout the Mediterranean. Sometime around 1200 BC, the Mycenaean palaces were

A piece of a Mycenaean pot with a vigorous dancing scene.

destroyed, for reasons that remain unclear, and cultural development declined. The epic poems of **Homer**, written more than 400 years later, recall the glory of the Mycenaean age and may have their origins in this late **Bronze Age** society.

*These blue glass beads are from a tomb at **Mycenae**. They show that the Mycenaeans knew how to make glass objects in moulds. Each bead is in the shape of a vase and was covered in a thin sheet of gold.*

Myth

Myths are stories that played an important part in Greek thought and **religion**. The myths come from an age when there was no writing. Stories were passed from one generation to the next by means of an oral tradition, that is, storytelling by word of mouth. Many myths are about a magical age of heroes and great deeds. Perhaps some of them are a distant memory of the prosperous **Mycenaean civilization**, while many serve to explain features of the landscape and local history. For example, the highest mountain in mainland Greece, Mount **Olympus**, became the home of the gods, and Athens was named in honour of the goddess **Athena**.

At a deeper level, myths served as a way of thinking about the world and the powerful forces that govern human lives. Strong emotions like jealousy, love and hate were explored in myths such as those of **Orestes** and **Medea**.

Greek myths reflect the sense that there is an inevitable **fate** controlling humanity. Yet, at the same time, people could never know what fate held in store for them, so that life seemed very uncertain and unpredictable. Sometimes in Greek myths the gods behave in a very human way, but they are also immortal, all-powerful, and look upon mortals with a mixture of sympathy and contempt.

Social and political ideas, such as the relationship between the individual and the state, are embedded in myths like that of **Oedipus** and his daughter Antigone. Greek playwrights in their **drama** often explored these kinds of myths. Myths served different purposes and this helps explain why there are different versions of the same story, as in the tale of **Iphigenia**. One version has a tragic ending but the other version ends happily.

Greek **myths** have remained popular over the centuries. These porcelain vases were made by the Sèvres company in France in about 1780. Both vases have painted panels showing scenes from Greek mythology. The one on the right shows **Aphrodite** and **Adonis**.

Nakedness

Men in ancient Greece had a very relaxed attitude towards nakedness, and the warm climate did not encourage them to wear a lot of clothes. Greek **women** were expected to keep their bodies covered, but men took nakedness among themselves for granted. Men took part in **wrestling**, **boxing** and other forms of **athletics** in the nude. Greek art, especially **sculpture**, often sought to portray the natural beauty of the human body.

Nakedness was normal for Greek athletes. The artist has caught the steady rhythm of the three runners. Their low leg and arm movements show they are running in a long-distance race, not a sprint.

*This pot shows the winged **Eros** with Peleus, the father of **Achilles**, and naked Thetis. It is quite unusual for a Greek pot to show a woman naked and men dressed.*

Narcissus (Narkissos)

In myth, Narcissus was a beautiful young man who showed no interest in the many girls and boys who fell in love with him. When Narcissus rejected the **nymph** Echo she was so upset that she withdrew from the world and pined away in a lonely spot until all that was left of her was her voice.

Other would-be lovers who had been rejected by Narcissus called on the gods for vengeance. This came about one hot day when Narcissus was looking into a stream. He fell deeply in love with his own reflection. He could not stop looking at himself and let himself die or, in another version of the story, killed

himself. On the spot where he died a white flower grew and was named after him. Narcissus has also entered our language in the word 'narcissism', meaning an obsession with one's own body and appearance.

Navy

The **Mediterranean** Sea was very important to the Greeks, so it is not surprising that ships and navies played an important role in Greek life. The Greek fighting ship was the trireme. A trireme had a crew of about 200 men. It was a costly business for any state to keep a navy. The crews had to be paid and the wood needed to build ships was in short supply.

The power and prestige of **Athens** was mainly due to its ability to maintain a large navy of some 200 ships. The Athenian navy defeated the Persians at the battle of **Salamis**. The wood needed to build ships was imported from **Thrace**. Athens paid for its navy with income from the state-owned silver mines and the tributes collected from states in the **Athenian Empire**.

The rowers who made up the navy did not have the social prestige of hoplites (see **armour and arms**). Rowers tended to come from among the poorer citizens, but their importance to the security of Athens made them politically strong.

Corinth, Aegina and other states had their own navies but none could match Athens, until Athens lost three-quarters of its fleet attacking **Sicily**. **Sparta** then developed its own navy and defeated its rival Athens in the **Peloponnesian War**.

Nemesis

Nemesis was a goddess who carried out vengeance on behalf of the gods. She punished mortals who dared to overstep their limits as mere humans, and so were guilty of **hubris**. Nemesis was an important concept for the Greeks but, like hubris, it is not easy to translate it into English. It represents an attitude of mind that belongs to an ancient society some 2,500 years ago. **Croesus** suffered nemesis after he had acted as if he was invincible. The playwright **Aeschylus**, in his play *Persians*, showed **Xerxes** meeting the same fate because of his proud ambition to conquer the world.

*An engraved gem showing **Nike** erecting a trophy.*

Nike

Nike, the goddess of victory, was a daughter of Titans (see **creation myth**) who fought against them on the side of **Zeus**. She was not only connected with military victories, but was popularly depicted in art as associated with other kinds of contests, such as **athletics** and **music**. Nike is often shown with two wings as a symbol of speed

*A bronze figurine of **Nike**.*

and victory rather than a goddess with a personality of her own. In **Athens**, the celebration of Nike merged with the worship of **Athena**.

Nymphs

Nymphs were spirits of nature who lived in the countryside. They were part of the bounty and beauty of nature and, like fairies or leprechauns in other cultures, they shied away from contact with people. They were the mortal daughters of **Zeus**, young and beautiful, and capable of inspiring other mortals with their love of music and dancing.

Nymphs were often associated with a particular cave, river or other local place, and they were known by a variety of names. Usually they were kind to humans, and were linked with **Asclepius** and the healing of the sick, but they were also associated with **satyrs** and with **Dionysus** and the wilder aspects of nature. **Calypso** and Echo (see **Narcissus**) were both nymphs.

*Two **nymphs** painted on a red-figure pot.*

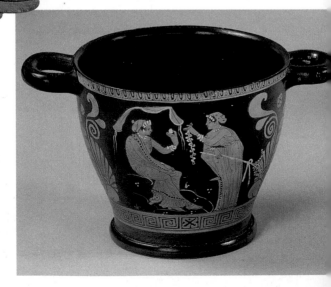

Odysseus

Odysseus was a legendary hero who left his home to fight at **Troy**. He was the king of Ithaca, husband to **Penelope** and father of Telemachus. Odysseus was the most famous of all Greek heroes, but at first he did not want to fight. To try to escape service, he pretended to be mad by ploughing the sandy beach and sowing it with salt. However, the trick failed when his baby son Telemachus was placed in front of the plough. Odysseus revealed his sanity by stopping the plough before it could hurt the boy.

Despite his reluctance to fight, Odysseus became a renowned warrior at Troy, combining physical strength and bravery with wisdom and intelligence. He disguised himself as a deserter and entered Troy to persuade **Helen** to betray the city. It was also Odysseus who came up with the idea of capturing the city by means of a **Wooden Horse**. When the war was over, Odysseus set off for home but it took ten years and many adventures before he was reunited with Penelope and Telemachus. These adventures make up the story of Homer's **Odyssey**.

Odysseus, with the aid of a companion, blinds Polyphemus the Cyclops.

Odyssey

The *Odyssey* was one of the two great epic poems by **Homer**. It was written down in the mid-8th century BC although it certainly comes from an earlier tradition of poetry that was oral (spoken, not written). The story harks back to the earlier age of heroes and the culture of the **Bronze Age**. The *Odyssey* tells the story of the return home of the Greek hero **Odysseus** after the end of the war at **Troy**. However, Odysseus does not appear in the first books of the poem. These deal with the attempts of his wife Penelope and son Telemachus to keep control of their kingdom in his absence.

On their homeward voyage, Odysseus and his men land in a country where the inhabitants feed them lotus flowers, making them want to stay there and forget their mission. Odysseus forces them to leave. After escaping from the cave of Polyphemus, one of the **Cyclopes**, Odysseus arrives on the island of Aeolus, the keeper of the winds.

Aeolus gives Odysseus a bag containing all the winds except one, to help him sail back home. But, within sight of Ithaca, the sailors open the bag hoping to find gold. Instead the winds escape and they are blown off course to land in the country of the Laestrygonians. Here, their ships are attacked and Odysseus manages to escape with just one ship and its crew. They sail on to the island where the sorceress **Circe** lives and she directs Odysseus to the coast of the Underworld to seek advice on how to return home.

The next adventure involves the **Sirens**, who lure sailors to their deaths. After this Odysseus and his crew have to navigate a narrow strait of water between the multi-headed sea monster Scylla on one side and the whirlpool of Charybdis on the other. Scylla snatches some of the crew but the survivors escape to the island of Helios, the sun god. There,

*This terracotta from the 5th century BC depicts Scylla, described in the **Odyssey** as having six heads, each of which has three rows of teeth 'thick and close and full of black death'.*

rescued by a servant and brought up by the king and queen of **Corinth** as their own son.

When Oedipus grew up he went to the **oracle** at **Delphi**, which told him he would kill his father and marry his mother. Hoping to avoid these sins, Oedipus left Corinth and headed towards Thebes. On the road there he happened to meet his real father and, without realizing who he was, killed him after an argument.

At that time Thebes was being terrorized by the Sphinx, a monster that

against the orders of Odysseus, the men kill and eat the god's cattle. Helios calls on **Zeus** for **revenge** and only Odysseus escapes with his life when his ship is struck by lightning. Swept into the sea, he finally reaches **Calypso**'s island, where he has to stay for seven years. At last he builds a raft and eventually sails home to Ithaca.

The *Odyssey* concludes with the story of how Odysseus defeated **Penelope**'s suitors, who were trying to take his kingdom. After a separation of twenty years, she did not recognize the disguised Odysseus until he proved himself to her by revealing a secret only he could know.

Oedipus (Oidipous)

The name Oedipus means 'swollen foot'. Oedipus was born under a curse that he would kill his father, the king of **Thebes**. When Oedipus was a tiny baby his father left him exposed on a mountainside to die. His ankles were pierced so that they could be tied together, but he was

__Oedipus__ explaining the riddle of the Sphinx. This painting is by Ingres, a French artist of the 19th century AD.

was half-lion and half-woman. The Sphinx asked each person it encountered a riddle: 'What walks on four legs in the morning, two at noon and three at the end of day?' Anyone who could not answer the riddle – and up to then no one could – was eaten by the Sphinx. Oedipus met the Sphinx and solved the riddle. The answer was a man, who crawls on all fours as a baby, later walks on two legs, and then in old age – the twilight years – walks with a stick for support.

The Sphinx killed itself, and the Thebans were so happy at being saved from the monster that they gave Oedipus the throne and the hand of their widowed queen in marriage. Thus the prophecy was fulfilled, because Jocasta, the queen, was his mother.

Later, a plague came to Thebes and it was foretold that the plague would end if the murderer of the last king could be identified. Oedipus started investigating how the king had died and eventually discovered the awful truth for himself. Jocasta hanged herself in grief and Oedipus blinded himself and went into **exile** with his daughter Antigone.

Oligarchy

Oligarchy, a Greek word meaning 'rule by the few', is a form of **government** and it was common in ancient Greece. Unlike a **democracy**, an oligarchy excluded the majority of the citizens from taking part in government. A minority of men from rich families controlled the state.

Sparta championed oligarchies while **Athens** promoted democracy. However, even in Athens there were unsuccessful attempts at establishing oligarchies. During the **Peloponnesian War**, in 411 BC a group of rich families in Athens dismantled the democracy and governed the city. They were known as the Four Hundred. They were deposed in the same year, but when Sparta defeated

Athens in 404 BC, the Spartans set up another oligarchy, known as the Thirty Tyrants. Democracy was later restored in Athens, but oligarchy became more common in the **Hellenistic Age**.

Olives

Olives (see also **farming**) were of special importance to the Greeks. Even though olives were not eaten raw, they could be processed for a variety of purposes. They were crushed and pressed, without breaking the stones in the olives, to make oil. Olive oil was used as **food**; in place of

Olives *were the most important part of the Athenian economy and were its largest export.*

soap; as a fuel for lamps; and for rubbing on the body during competitions and training for **athletics**.

Olive trees are easy to grow, but it takes fifteen years to yield the first crop and forty years for a tree to reach maturity. Even then, it only bears a crop every second year. Once mature, though, trees last for hundreds of years. The long roots of the olive tree allow it to absorb water from deep underground and survive the long dry summers of the Greek **climate**. The olive tree cannot flourish on high ground because frosts will kill it. The most northerly Greek colonies around the Black Sea and in the north Aegean are the farthest north that olives will grow.

Olive oil was exported in amphorae – clay pots – from different parts of Greece. Some regions, such as Attica, around **Athens**, and the island of Samos, became well known for their high-quality oil. The olive was an important symbol to the Athenians. Victors at the **Panathenaea** were rewarded with oil from the sacred trees given to the city by **Athena**. Something similar occurred at the **Olympic Games**.

Olympic Games

The Olympic Games were the most important and oldest sports event of the ancient Greeks, who traced back the first Games to 776 BC. The Games were part of an important religious **festival** in honour of **Zeus**. By the 7th century BC the event was so important that a truce was declared by states at **war**, while the Games were in progress, so that nothing could prevent athletes from journeying to Olympia in the Peloponnese.

The athletic events were open to all Greek men – but not slaves. However, only rich aristocrats could afford the time to train and travel to major athletic events such as the Games. Thus, the Games also acted as a meeting place for

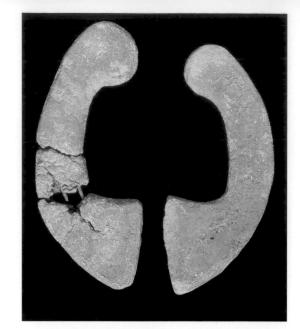

*These jumping weights weigh just over 1 kg (2 lbs) each and are 19 cm (7.5 inches) in length. Nobody knows if Greek athletes in the jumping events at the **Olympic Games** took a run-up or jumped from a standing start.*

*An athlete in the starting position for a running race at the **Olympic Games**.*

various noble families from across Greece, who, like most aristocracies, were often connected through marriage.

The Games took place every four years and lasted five days. The victors were crowned with a wreath of laurel leaves, but they could expect much richer rewards, including a pension for life, when they returned home to their **city-states**. A city-state could give the equivalent of £300,000 (US$500,000) to a victor, who could also look forward to great success in society or in politics.

In line with the ancient Greek attitude to **competition**, winning was everything at the Olympic Games. There were no prizes or recognition for those who came second or third in an event. Women took part in separate games at

*Left: on the first day of the **Olympic Games**, competitions were held to choose the trumpeters who signalled the start of events. The trumpeters also announced the results of previous competitions. This bronze figure was crafted in the 5th century BC, although the trumpet may be modern.*

*Below: the modern **Olympic Games** begin with an international celebration. The original Olympic Games began with sacrifices to the gods.*

Olympia, called the Heraea in honour of the goddess **Hera**, though there was only one running event.

The first modern Olympic Games took place in Athens in 1896. They concluded with the marathon race, celebrating the journey run by an Athenian messenger after victory at the Battle of **Marathon**. The event was won by Spiridon Louis, a Greek shepherd.

Olympus (Olympos)

At 2,918 metres (9,573 feet), Mount Olympus is the highest mountain in mainland Greece. It is situated in the north of the country in **Thessaly**. In myth, Mount Olympus was the home of **Zeus** and the other important gods. They were known as the Olympian gods. From the summit of the mountain, often shrouded in mist, Zeus and his fellow gods would look down on the world of mortals below.

*This pot shows the gods of **Olympus** battling with their traditional enemies, the giants.*

*Below: Mount **Olympus**, home of the ancient Greek gods and goddesses.*

Oracles

Oracles offered a way for human beings to ask questions of the gods. Oracles played an important role in Greek **religion**, but interpreting the words of the gods could be a tricky business. **Croesus**, the wealthy king of **Lydia**, found out the hard way that the oracle's response could have more than one meaning. The oracle told Croesus that if he fought the Persians, he would bring down a mighty empire. Croesus, encouraged, went to war, but the Persians defeated him. The mighty empire that fell was his own. **Oedipus** was also told the truth by the oracle – he would murder his father and marry his mother – but by trying to avoid this he actually brought it about.

Ordinary people consulted oracles over everyday matters. Questions have been found asking which god might improve the pilgrim's eyesight, or what had happened to someone's bedclothes that had mysteriously disappeared. At **Delphi**, the most famous site of an oracle, questions for the god **Apollo** were written down and handed to an attendant. The prophecy was delivered by a priestess in a state of trance. The words of the god were put into lines of verse and given to the pilgrim by the attendant.

The oracle of Dodona, in the far northwest of Greece, took the form of an oak tree. It not clear how the tree 'spoke'. A priestess may have interpreted the rustling of leaves or the flight of birds from its branches. Another famous oracle was at Siwa in the desert of **Egypt**. According to **Alexander the Great**, the oracle here declared him a living god.

The French artist Claude Lorraine drew this picture of Delphi, home of the famous **oracle**, *in the 17th century* AD

Orestes

Orestes was the son of **Agamemnon** and Clytemnestra. He felt bound to take revenge on Clytemnestra after she killed his father. Then Orestes was pursued by the Furies for mudering his mother. The goddess Athena finally saved Orestes and brought about a peaceful resolution. See also **Electra** and **Aeschylus**.

Orpheus

In myth, Orpheus was a gifted singer and musician from **Thrace** whose music could charm wild animals, violent men and even the trees and stones. He accompanied **Jason and the Argonauts**

Orpheus playing his lyre between two Thracians. The Muses taught Orpheus to play.

and, in one story of their adventures, he sang to calm the crew and the waves in a storm. Later he saved the crew from the **Sirens** because his voice and playing were more beautiful than theirs. Misfortune came to him when his wife **Eurydice** died. Orpheus travelled to **Hades** to rescue her, but he had to return without her because he looked back at her before they had left the Underworld. Orpheus was killed by the women of Thrace. Different versions of the story give different reasons why. His body was torn to pieces and his head was thrown into a river. It floated down, still singing, to the sea.

In **religion** a cult belief developed known as Orphism, based on the visit to Hades by Orpheus. The belief was that after death the soul passed to another life form until eventually it reached a state of heavenly bliss.

Ostracism

Ostracism means excluding someone from society, usually by refusing to have anything to do with them. The term comes from the Athenians' system of banishing a person from their **city-state** for a period of ten years.

Once a year, **citizens** would write the name of the politician they wanted banished on a piece of broken pottery, called an *ostrakon*. Anyone receiving 6,000 votes, or the person with the most votes over 6,000, was given ten days to pack up and leave. Their property was not confiscated and they could return to political life after the ten years, but their political careers were usually broken.

Ostracism was also practised in some other city-states, including **Miletus**. In a colony in **Sicily** there was a similar system, called petalism, in which the names were written on olive leaves (*petala*).

Painting

Evidence of the history of Greek painting goes back to the Mycenaean and Archaic times, when walls and vases were covered in patterns and scenes from **myth** and everyday life. In the **Classical Age** artists painted on wooden panels with a white background, but hardly any examples have survived. Greek **sculptures** were painted, but none of the original paint survives. Nobody is certain whether statues were completely painted in gaudy reds, yellows, greens and blues or whether colour was added more discreetly. Brightly coloured paints were used to highlight and decorate parts of buildings, but we do not know exactly how this was done. Paintings on wood were displayed in the **agora** at **Athens**. Artists also painted backdrops for the **theatre**. Today few Greek paintings survive except paintings on **pottery**. From the vase-paintings we can see the level of skill and artistry achieved by Greek artists.

*Three examples of white-ground pots from the 5th century BC. The colours used to paint the pots may be similar to those used on wall-**paintings** and on sculptures.*

*This silver tray was made by a Roman craftsman in the 4th century AD. The rim shows the Greek god **Pan** (with the legs of a goat and holding a reed pipe) with **Dionysus**, **maenads** and **satyrs**.*

Pan

Pan was a god of flocks and of fertility and a protector of shepherds. He had a human body but the legs, ears and horns of a goat. He was bearded, played a reed pipe (also called a pan-pipe), was swift of foot and chased the **nymphs**. Pan was a son of **Hermes** and lived in remote regions of mountains and caves, such as

*In this painting, The Triumph of Pan, the cloven-hoofed **Pan** is in the centre. In the foreground you can see a set of pan-pipes and masks from a drama. Nicolas Poussin painted this picture in the 17th century AD.*

Arcadia, where the worship of Pan originated. When news came that the Persians had landed at **Marathon**, a messenger named Pheidippides was sent from **Athens** to ask **Sparta** for help. It is said that Pheidippides covered the 240 kilometres (150 miles) in just two days and that, on his way, he was inspired by a meeting with Pan.

Panathenaea

The Panathenaea was a major **festival** celebrated each year in **Athens** in honour of the birth of the goddess **Athena**. Every four years it was a bigger event than usual and was called the Great Panathenaea. There were animal

sacrifices, sports competitions and a procession. At the Panathenaea a sleeveless garment called a *peplos* (see **clothes**) was carried in a special cart and then presented to the colossal statue of the goddess inside the temple. The annual festival also served to celebrate the Athenian state and everyone could join in, including women, non-Greeks and even slaves. The grand procession was the subject of sculptures in the **Parthenon**.

Pandora

Pandora was the world's first woman. A story says that she was created by **Zeus** and the other gods to plague men as a punishment. Zeus was angry with **Prometheus**, who had tricked him and shown favour to mortals. Prometheus had a brother called Epimetheus, whose name means 'think later'. He married Pandora even though he had been warned never to accept a gift from the gods. Pandora either brought with her, or found in the home of Epimetheus, a large storage jar. It contained all the evils of the world and just one good: Hope. Overcome by curiosity, Pandora took the lid off the jar and released evil into the world, leaving only Hope at the bottom.

Above: a scene from the frieze on the Parthenon temple shows the handing over of the peplos *during the* **Panathenaea** *festival.*

Below: this scene from a wine bowl shows **Athena** *preparing* **Pandora** *for her arrival among men. Pandora stands stiffly, as if she is not fully human yet.*

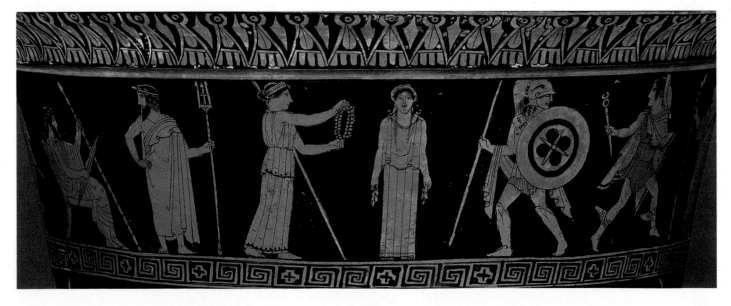

Paris

In myth, Paris was a prince of **Troy**, the son of King Priam and Queen Hecuba and brother to **Hector**. He won the love of **Helen**, the wife of King Menelaus of Sparta, and took her back to Troy. This started the **Trojan War**. The goddess **Aphrodite** had promised to give Helen to Paris if he judged her the winner of a beauty contest between the Olympian goddesses. The losers, **Hera** and **Athena,** were so jealous that they both became enemies of Troy.

It was Paris who killed the mighty **Achilles**, shooting an arrow that struck him in his vulnerable heel. Paris himself was later shot by a Greek warrior called Philoctetes. The wounded Paris could have been saved by the healing power of Oenone, a **nymph** whom he had loved but deserted for Helen. Oenone delayed and Paris died before she finally arrived.

*This watercolour painting by William Blake shows **Paris** judging the beauty contest between the goddesses. Paris chooses **Aphrodite** as the most beautiful. He is handing her a golden apple.*

112

Parthenon

The Parthenon is a **temple** to **Athena** built on the **Acropolis** at Athens in 447–432 BC. It stands near the site of an earlier temple to Athena, which had been destroyed by the **Persians**.

The Parthenon was built at the height of Athens' prosperity, by the best available architects and artists, including **Phidias**. It is still standing some two-and-a-half thousand years later, despite severe damage caused by an explosion in a war in 1687 and the disappearance of its roof.

The core of the temple is divided into two rooms. Phidias made a colossal statue of Athena 10.5 metres (35 feet) high to stand in the main room. It was made of a framework covered in ivory (for the flesh parts) and gold (for the drapery). She held a human-sized statue of the goddess **Nike** in her right hand.

The temple building measures 69 metres (228 feet) by 31 metres (101 feet) and is made of marble. It was once richly decorated with sculptures both inside and out. Many of the sculptures were removed in 1801 and eventually sold to the British Museum (see **Elgin Marbles**).

The temple's frieze showed the

*The **Parthenon** temple (left) as it stands today. The carved horsemen (above) come from the frieze that ran round the Parthenon, inside the portico. The sculptures were originally painted in bright colours.*

Did You Know?

The columns of the Parthenon lean inwards slightly to avoid the appearance of top-heaviness. If the columns were extended they would eventually meet 2.5 kilometres ($1\frac{1}{2}$ miles) up in the sky.

procession of the annual Panathenaic festival. Rectangular panels on the outside of the temple, called metopes, showed sculptures in relief. The Parthenon metopes depicted battles between **Centaurs** and the Lapiths, a people of **Thessaly**, as well as fights between gods and giants, Greeks and Trojans, and Greeks and Amazons.

The Parthenon's pediments, the triangular parts above the columns at the front and back of the temple, showed sculptures of the birth of Athena and the contest between Athena and **Poseidon** for influence over Athens.

Pegasus

Pegasus was a winged horse that played a part in the myths of **Perseus** and Bellerophon. Pegasus was born in the far west of the known world, springing from the neck of the decapitated Gorgon **Medusa**, after Perseus slew her. In another version, he was born from the

Above: a coin showing **Pegasus**. *The winged horse often appeared on early coins from Corinth.*

Right: **Pegasus** *and Bellerophon defeating the Chimaera, a monster with a lion's head, a goat's head and a serpent for a tail.*

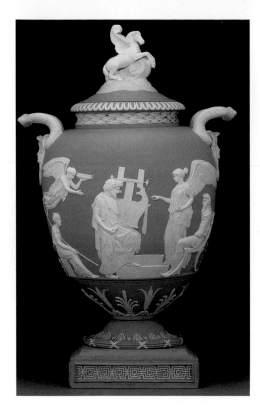

earth where Medusa's blood was spilt. Pegasus was ridden by the hero Bellerophon who, with the help of the winged horse, survived various adventures including a fight with the monstrous Chimaera. But when Bellerophon tried to use Pegasus to climb high into the sky, the realm of the gods, he was thrown off.

*Josiah Wedgwood made this vase in the 18th century AD. It is called the **Pegasus Vase**, after the winged horse on the lid. The man with the lyre is **Homer**.*

Peloponnesian War

The Peloponnesian War was a struggle between **Athens** and **Sparta**. It involved allies on both sides and lasted on and off for twenty-seven years. The war started when Athens and Corcyra allied themselves against **Corinth**. However, the real cause of the war was a power struggle between Athens and Sparta. Athens was backed by the states of the **Athenian Empire**, while Sparta was supported by most of its neighbouring states in the Peloponnese (the large peninsula of southern Greece).

The war began in 431 BC and dragged on inconclusively. Athens was strong at sea, but Sparta was superior on land, so neither side could achieve a decisive victory. Under the leadership of **Pericles,** Athens mostly pursued a defensive policy. The enemy was allowed to invade Athenian territory while people took refuge within the city and inside the Long Walls that connected Athens with the port of Piraeus some 6 kilometres (4 miles) away.

Athens could rely on its navy to protect its lines of supply. But, when the Spartan army was outside the city walls, so many people crowded into the city and the Long Walls for protection that a terrible plague broke out. Sparta gained an edge in the war after Athens failed to conquer **Sicily** in 413 BC. The next year, Sparta allied itself with **Persia** and built a fleet. Athens could not withstand these odds and finally surrendered in 404 BC.

*The Long Walls of **Athens** were destroyed by **Sparta** after their victory in the **Peloponnesian War**. The walls were later rebuilt, but no trace of them remains today.*

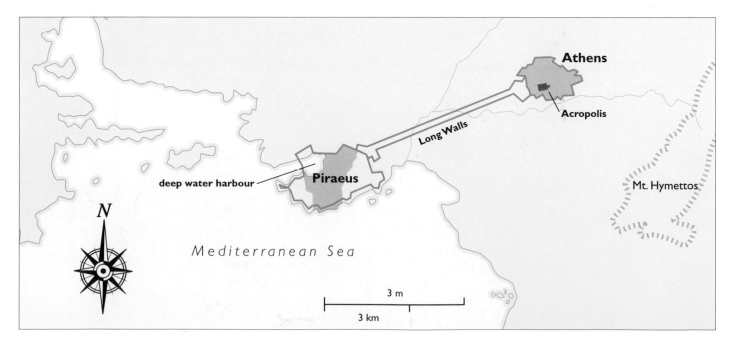

Penelope

In myth, Penelope was the wife of the Greek hero **Odysseus**. For twenty years she loyally waited for him to return from Troy to their home in Ithaca. Homer's **Odyssey** tells how, during that time, she was pestered by many suitors who wished to marry her and gain the family's land.

For a long time Penelope kept the suitors at bay by claiming she could not marry until she had finished weaving a shroud. Each night she secretly unravelled her day's work so the shroud was never finished. After a while the suitors discovered her trick.

Penelope then said she would marry anyone who could string the mighty bow of her Odysseus and fire an arrow through the empty sockets of a dozen axe heads lined up straight. This amazing feat was achieved by Odysseus himself, who had returned home in disguise. He killed all the suitors and was reunited with Penelope.

Pericles (Perikles)

Pericles (495–429 BC) was a great politician from Athens. He influenced many aspects of his city's development. He was a supporter of democracy and that made him popular with the poorer citizens. He promoted the payment of jurors in the law courts and successfully urged his fellow citizens to beautify their city with an expensive programme of public buildings on the Acropolis. Pericles also urged the building of the Long Walls to link Athens with her port (see page 115). The Long Walls became very important during the Peloponnesian War against Sparta. Pericles also played an influential role in persuading Athens to go to war with Sparta. It was his idea for the Athenians to stay inside the city walls and allow the Spartan army to devastate the countryside. Pericles had a reputation for never smiling and was said to have wept only twice in his life.

*This pot shows **Perseus** (on the left) just after killing the Gorgon **Medusa**. He has her head in a bag slung from his shoulder. His patron goddess Athena stands on the right.*

Perseus

In myth, Perseus was the son of **Zeus** and the princess Danaë of Argos. Earlier, her father, King Acrisius, had been warned that he would be killed by his own grandson. Consequently, he kept his daughter a prisoner, but Zeus visited her in the form of a shower of gold and she later gave birth to Perseus. Danaë's father put them out to sea in a chest. They were washed up on the island of Seriphus, where the king wanted to force Danaë to marry him. To get rid of Perseus, the king set him the seemingly impossible task of killing the Gorgon **Medusa**. However, Perseus succeeded, and he returned home with the princess **Andromeda** whom he had rescued on the way. He saved his mother by using the Gorgon's head to turn the king into stone. Perseus then tried to find his grandfather Acrisius, but accidentally killed him with a discus. So the prophecy came true.

Persia

Persia developed one of the greatest empires of the ancient world. It was formed by Cyrus the Great in the 6th century BC. The empire grew under the kings Cambyses and Darius, stretching as far as **Asia Minor** in the west, Pakistan in the east, **Egypt** in the south and the Black Sea in the north. It was so large that it took three months to travel from the capital at Susa to the coast of Asia Minor. To govern such a vast area, the empire was divided into provinces, called satrapies. Each satrapy had its own ruler who reported to Susa.

Persia's ambition to conquer Greece led to the **Persian Wars**. In the end Persia did not succeed in its aim, and the

*At its height, the empire of **Persia** stretched from Greek Asia Minor to the River Indus in the east. The scale gives some idea of its enormous size.*

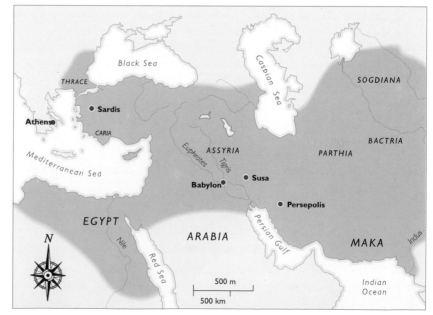

A scene from the **Persian Wars**. A Greek hoplite, or foot soldier, engages a mounted Persian soldier in battle. The Greek has bare arms and legs and a metal helmet while the Persian is dressed in an oriental style.

Persian empire was decisively defeated when **Alexander the Great** invaded it in 334 BC.

Persian Wars

The Persian Wars were two attempts by the mighty empire of **Persia** to conquer the much smaller and disunited states of Greece.

The first attempt followed a revolt by **Ionia** in 499 BC against Persian rule. Both **Athens** and the neighbouring island state of Eretria gave support to the rebels. The Persian king, Darius, was so annoyed by this that he ordered a servant to whisper to him each evening at dinner 'Remember the Athenians'. So Darius decided to conquer Greece.

Persian messengers were sent to Greek states demanding tokens of earth and water, the traditional symbols of submission. Athens refused, as did **Sparta**. The Spartans even threw the messengers down a well, where they said the Persians would find plenty of earth and water.

In 490 BC the Persians led a seaborne invasion and crushed Eretria, before being humiliatingly defeated by the Athenians at the Battle of **Marathon**.

Ten years later the son of Darius, **Xerxes**, sought revenge by sending a great navy and a huge army of hundreds of thousands of soldiers. He crossed the Hellespont, the narrow strait of water between Asia and Europe, by means of two bridges made of boats. After the invasion, the Greeks fought the Persians at **Thermopylae** and defeated their navy at **Salamis**. Xerxes returned to Susa but left an army in Greece, which was later destroyed at the battle of **Plataea**.

Phidias (Pheidias)

Phidias was an artist and sculptor from **Athens**. He created the chryselephantine (gold and ivory) statue of **Athena** for the **Parthenon**.

He first made a framework and then covered the head and limbs in ivory. He covered the body with plates of gold that had been shaped in clay moulds so that Athena was draped in shining metal. Phidias used the same method to create a colossal statue of Zeus at Olympia, one of the Seven Wonders of the Ancient World.

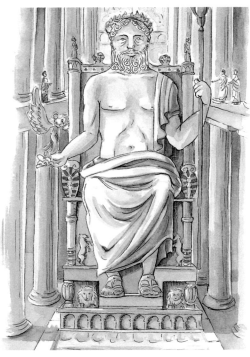

An artist's reconstruction of the statue of Zeus at Olympia made by **Phidias**.

Pheidippides

Pheidippides was the Athenian messenger who ran to request Spartan help in 490 BC when the Persians landed at **Marathon**.

It was said that he was given the strength to complete his great journey by an encounter with the god **Pan**.

Wise Words of Wise Philosophers

'If you will take my advice, you will think little of Socrates and a great deal more of truth.'

Socrates

'Everything is becoming, nothing is.'

Plato

'What is being?'

Aristotle

'Men are good in one way, but bad in another'.

Aristotle

A **Phoenician** *galley, from a carving at the palace of the Assyrian king Sennacherib. The Phoenicians traded with the Greeks but their ships would also have fought against the Greeks during the* **Persian Wars**.

Philosophy

Philosophy is an ancient Greek word meaning 'a love of wisdom'. Philosophy is the study of life and its meaning and purpose. The first philosophers, known as the **Pre-Socratics**, investigated natural phenomena. Greek thinkers such as **Socrates**, **Plato** and **Aristotle** have had an enormous influence on philosophy in later centuries.

Phoenicia

Phoenicia (see map, page 5) was a land in the eastern **Mediterranean**, where modern Lebanon is today. The Phoenician people, who were not Greeks, developed the art of **seafaring** and traded with early Greece from the 10th century BC. The Phoenicians influenced Greek culture in many ways. The Greeks adapted their script to make an alphabet for their **language**, and learned new ideas from them

that found their way into Greek **religion**, **myth** and art forms such as **sculpture**. In the 6th century BC, Phoenicia was conquered by **Persia** and remained under Persian rule until the time of **Alexander the Great**.

Plataea

Plataea, a town in central Greece, was the scene of two battles. In 479 BC the battle of Plataea was the final and conclusive battle of the **Persian Wars**. After the Persian navy had been defeated, the Persian king returned home but left his army under the command of Mardonius to mount an attack once winter was over. Persia had a Greek ally in the city of **Thebes** and their joint armies marched south in the spring of 479. Near the town of Plataea they engaged the Greeks. After days of skirmishing the Persians attacked, using their powerful cavalry to good effect. However they could not match the Greek foot soldiers. Following the death of Mardonius, the Persians withdrew but were massacred by the Greeks.

During the **Peloponnesian War**, Thebes laid siege to Plataea for two years and eventually the troops defending it were massacred.

Plato

Plato was the first Greek philosopher whose complete works in the original language have survived. He was a great original thinker and his contribution to **philosophy** remains enormously influential. He lived around 427–347 BC in **Athens**, and founded the world's first university there. Over its doors were the words: 'Let no one enter here who is ignorant of geometry'. In universities today Plato's works are still studied.

Plato developed the idea that behind the world of everyday reality there are eternal Forms. For example, what we call the colour of blood resembles the Form of Redness. He applied the same idea to concepts like Justice and Truth and tried to establish through reason and argument what was the nature of these

Forms. As a young philosopher in Athens he was a pupil of **Socrates**. Observing Socrates' trial and execution may have influenced Plato to believe that the perfect form of government would be one run by philosophers.

Plato's most famous works include the *Republic*, *Apology*, *Phaedo* and *Symposium*. In some of them Socrates appears as a character arguing a philosophical point of view.

Poseidon

Poseidon was an ancient deity (see **creation myth**). He was the brother of **Zeus** and **Hades**, and he was worshipped throughout the Greek world as the god of the sea, the tamer of horses and the source of earthquakes. Fishermen and sailors looked to Poseidon for safe voyages. Not surprisingly, his most important temples were situated in coastal regions.

In **Athens** Poseidon had his own shrine on the **Acropolis**, even though in myth he disputed with the goddess **Athena** over whom the city should worship as their patron god. The struggle with Athena was represented in sculptures on the **Parthenon** temple. **Odysseus** received help from the goddess Athena, but Poseidon brought him nothing but bad luck.

Pottery

Pottery in the ancient world was used for a variety of everyday purposes. The clay was shaped on a potter's wheel and baked hard at a high temperature to make pots

*A Greek potter making **pottery** on a wheel.*

and other containers. A large two-handled pot, the amphora, was the common means of storing and transporting goods such as olive oil and grain. More expensive pots and jugs were prized items for the home.

Because pottery does not decay with age, it can be examined for its style and likely date of manufacture and then used by archaeologists to date sites. It is known, for example, that the colony of Naukratis in **Egypt** was founded towards the end of the 7th century BC, because this is the age of the oldest pottery found there by archaeologists. Around the 10th century BC a style called 'geometric' emerged in Greece. It featured geometric patterns and human stick figures. Other styles of painted pottery developed in **Corinth** in the 8th century BC.

By 600 BC Athens was beginning to produce black-figure pottery. Decorations were applied to pots, using a special clay mix called a gloss, which when heated turned black, leaving the background colour red or cream. The reverse method,

*Greek **pottery**. The first pot (**a**) was made in the 10th century BC, showing simple decoration of lines and circles. The second pair of pots (**b**) were made in the 8th or 7th centuries BC in the style called 'geometric' because of the geometric patterns. The third pot (**c**), depicting animals, was made in Corinth some 300 years later and shows the advance in pottery techniques.*

*The pot (**d**) is in the black-figure style, made in the middle of the 6th century BC. Pot (**e**), made in Athens about a hundred years later, is a red-figure pot showing two warriors.*

121

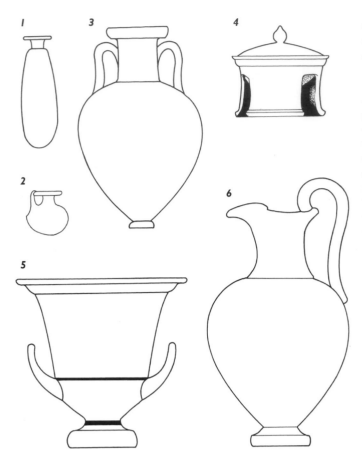

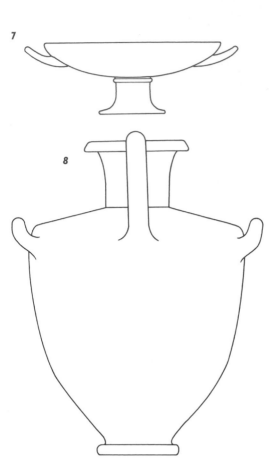

*Greek **pottery**. Pots had different shapes and sizes according to their function.*

__1__ is a small flask, an alabastron, for oil or perfume. __2__ is an aryballos, a small flask used by athletes for carrying oil. __3__ is a tall vessel with two handles, an amphora, used for storing and transporting wine, oil and other goods. __4__ is a cosmetic or jewellery box with a lid. __5__ is a krater and was used to mix water and wine. __6__ is a wine jug, called an oinochoe, and these came in a variety of shapes. __7__ is a kylix, a shallow drinking cup with handles. __8__ is a large three-handled pot called a hydria, used for storing water.

called red-figure pottery, developed later and was used to make some of the finest Greek pottery to have survived.

Greek pots, with their scenes of ordinary life and **myth**, are a huge source of information about ancient Greece.

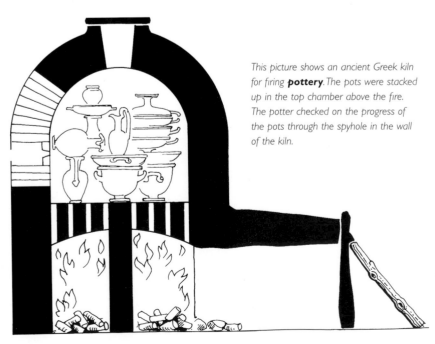

*This picture shows an ancient Greek kiln for firing **pottery**. The pots were stacked up in the top chamber above the fire. The potter checked on the progress of the pots through the spyhole in the wall of the kiln.*

Pre-Socratics

The Pre-Socratics were a group of philosophers and scientists who came from **Ionia** in the 6th century BC. Their great achievement was to apply method and reason, not **myth**, to speculation about the world and what is in it. **Thales**, Anaxagoras, **Anaximander** and **Heraclitus** all came up with different theories, but they shared a common desire to ask the same kind of questions – questions that ordinary Greeks did not ask. They are called Pre-Socratic because they came before the philosopher **Socrates**.

Priests and Priestesses

Generally, priests and priestesses were not full-time professionals. Their job was not to teach religious beliefs but to

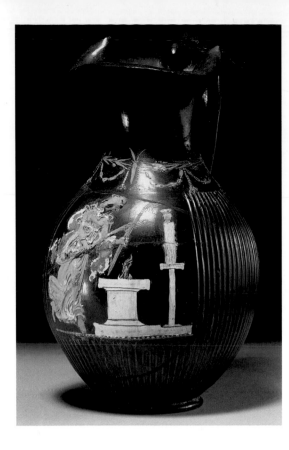

Left: this oinochoe *(wine jug) shows a* **priestess** *of Hecate at a shrine.*

Right: this painting by Moreau, a 19th-century AD *French painter, shows a strange-looking eagle tearing out the liver of* **Prometheus**.

perform rituals at **festivals** and in **temples** and to look after sacred objects placed in temples. The nearest equivalent to full-time professional priestesses and priests were the seers, or soothsayers, whose task it was to interpret messages and **prophecies** from the gods.

Prometheus

In myth, Prometheus was a Titan (see **creation myth**) who dared to help humankind and was punished severely for doing so.

Prometheus had to decide how a **sacrifice** should be made to the gods. He cut up a slaughtered bull, divided it into two parts and offered **Zeus** the choice of which part he wanted. The other part would be given to mortals, who at that time were only male. One share consisted of bones, disguised by being wrapped in fat, while the other share contained the meat parts wrapped inside the animal's stomach. Zeus chose the fatty portion, thinking the best parts lay under the fat. He was annoyed to discover he had only the bones to enjoy and took his revenge on mankind.

Zeus ordered the creation of womankind in the form of **Pandora** and he also withdrew fire from the use of man. Prometheus then stole fire from the gods and gave it to humans. Zeus punished him by chaining him to a rock where eagles came every day to eat his liver, which grew again overnight. Eventually, **Heracles** came and released Prometheus.

Prophecies

The Greeks looked for signs of communication from the gods. The task of interpreting such signs, or omens, belonged to the prophets and seers. They were important figures because the Greeks relied on omens to guide them before events such as battles or the founding of a **colony**. Seers would usually base their prophecies on an examination of the body organs of a sacrificed animal, or sometimes the flight patterns of birds. Prophetesses, or Sibyls, uttered or chanted aloud messages from the gods. The most important place for this activity was the **oracle** at the temple at **Delphi**.

Religion

Religion was one of the vitally important factors that gave ancient Greeks a sense of a shared identity. People all over the Greek world knew the same myths about gods and heroes, even though some cities and other places had special associations with particular **myths**. The same gods were worshipped with much the same rituals in **temples** that differed little from one part of the Greek world to another. Sacrificing animals, offering prayers and singing and dancing were common features of religious life. Certain beliefs, such as the use of **oracles**, were also shared. It was this common religion that drew participants from all over the Greek world to attend **festivals**.

Religion was not organized or experienced in the way modern religions are. There were no full-time **priests and priestesses**, no holy books like the Bible or Koran that laid down fixed beliefs. The gods were worshipped everywhere in the countryside: in caves, on mountain summits, in springs, on hillsides and elsewhere. Sacred acts, especially the making of **sacrifices**, were more at the heart of religion than the idea of individual holiness. **Magic** also played an important part in religion.

The gods of Greek religion did not represent ideas of goodness or perfection. They committed acts of violence, became jealous, committed adultery and could inflict pain and suffering on humans. The gods expected humans to offer them prayers and sacrifices, and in return mortals could ask for and expect their favours. However, not even the gods could override what **fate** had in store.

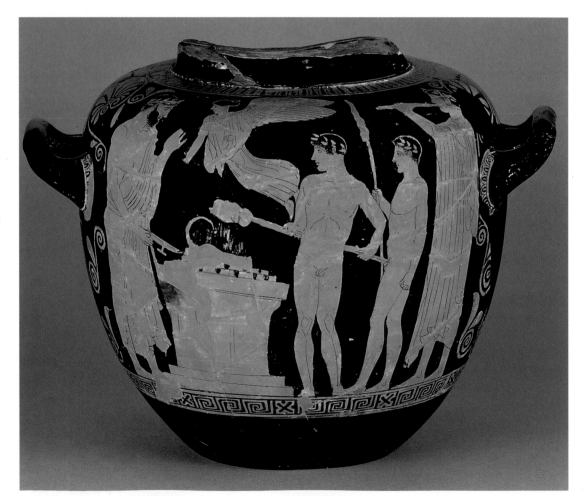

Religion was important in many aspects of Greek life. This pot shows victorious athletes at the Olympic Games making **sacrifices** to the gods.

Revenge

In the modern world, the wish to take revenge on someone is not usually seen as a good thing. To the Greeks revenge was an honourable aim. In a **law court** a prosecutor could justify bringing a case against someone by explaining that he was seeking revenge for a past wrong. This was understood and accepted. It was part of Greek thinking that anyone would want to harm his enemies and help his friends. The gods thought and acted in the same way and there are many stories, such as that of **Prometheus**, where a god seeks revenge.

Rome

The power of Rome was growing around the same time that the power of Greece was declining. In the last two centuries BC the Romans conquered the Greeks. In 30 BC the Romans conquered **Egypt**, where Greek remained the official **language**. In their conquest of the Greek world the Romans were deeply influenced by the culture of Greek civilization. They adopted many aspects of the Greek culture, including **religion** and the alphabet. They recognized what the Greeks had achieved, learned their language and read their literature. This prompted the Roman poet Horace to remark, 'Captive Greece took mighty Rome captive.'

*This Roman vase is an adaptation of a Greek-style vessel. It shows the influence of Greek art on the culture of **Rome**.*

Sacrifices

Making a sacrifice to the gods was the most important ritual in Greek **religion**. Sacrifices followed a set procedure. The highest form of sacrifice was to offer a bull, though a sheep or goat was more common and other domesticated animals could also be used. Flowers and cakes and other foods were also offered to the gods.

Inscriptions have survived explaining some of the reasons why offerings were made in ancient Greece. Sometimes people wanted to thank the god for a special favour, or to ask the god for something, or to mark a special family occasion like the birth of a child or a **marriage**.

A sacrifice began with a procession to the altar. The participants washed their hands, and shook water over the animal, compelling it to 'nod' in agreement to its sacrifice. Hair was cut from the animal and placed on the altar fire while the participants prayed and expressed their requests, or their thanks, to the gods. Barley grain was thrown over the animal, before it was stunned with a hard knock and its throat was cut. The blood was collected and poured onto the altar. The animal was then butchered, and the inedible thigh-bones were wrapped in fat and burned on the altar. It was **Prometheus** who first tricked the gods

*This section of the Parthenon frieze shows a heifer being led to **sacrifice** in the procession of the **Panathenaea**.*

480 BC. The citizens of Athens had deserted their city, knowing that the Persians were advancing on them after the Battle of **Thermopylae**. They relied on their **navy** to defeat the invaders. Their far-sighted leader Themistocles had persuaded them to spend a great deal of money on ships for the navy, because he foresaw the threat from Persia.

Before the battle of Salamis, Themistocles faced the problem of bringing the two sides together in water that favoured the Greeks. He persuaded the Greek admiral to keep the Greek fleet in the Bay of Salamis. At the same time he tricked the Persians into sailing into the narrow straits to attack. The Greek navy, trapped in the bay, had to fight fiercely. The Persians had more ships, but the Greek vessels were more seaworthy and had better crews.

The Persian king, **Xerxes**, watched the battle from a high point on the mainland. He saw to his horror that his large navy could not manoeuvre and fight effectively in the narrow channel. The Persians were defeated and Xerxes fled back to Asia across the Hellespont, leaving his army to be defeated by the Greeks at **Plataea**.

into accepting the inedible parts of the animal in their sacrifices. Wine was added to the fire, as an offering to the god. The edible parts of the animal were cooked and eaten by the human participants, providing them with a rare opportunity for a meat-based meal.

A libation was an offering of a liquid, usually **wine**, which could be poured on an altar, or over the ground, or left in a sacred spot. Some of the wine would usually be drunk by the participants.

The ancient Greeks did not carry out human sacrifice, although it occasionally occurs in myths (see **Iphigenia**).

*Above, A stone model of an altar. A fire is burning on top where the offerings of the **sacrifice** would be placed.*

Salamis

Salamis, an island to the west of **Athens** (see map, page 62), was the scene of a decisive sea battle in the **Persian Wars** in

Sappho

Sappho was a woman poet from the island of **Lesbos**. She was born around 630 BC and wrote love poetry to young women. Her poetry, which would have been spoken aloud to the accompaniment of lyre **music**, was much admired in her own time and still is today. Very little of her poetry has survived, but the fragments that have reveal a remarkable Greek woman.

One of her poems includes the lines 'Some say that a troop of cavalry is the most lovely sight on earth, some say that hoplites are, or some say ships of war, but I say it is the person you love.'

127

Satyrs

Satyrs were mythical spirits of the countryside. They had a mostly human appearance, but with some animal features such as long tails. Like **nymphs**, they were often associated with the god **Dionysus** and with wild behaviour. They were often portrayed on Greek vases, naked and goat-like, or sometimes horse-like, behaving in an unruly way.

*A seal stone with a picture of a **satyr** drinking. The Greek writer Hesiod said that the satyrs are the brothers of nymphs and are 'good-for-nothing and mischievous'.*

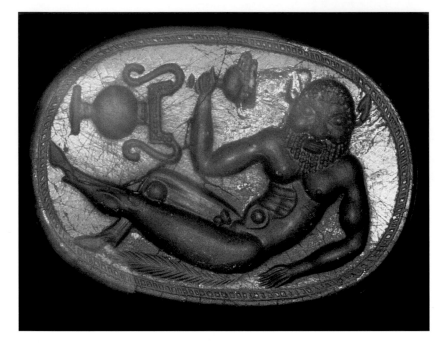

Sculpture

Sculpture was one of the most important arts in ancient Greece. Greek sculptures, made of marble, metal or limestone, are among the finest works of art ever produced and they have been admired and copied for centuries.

An early influence on Greek sculpture was the art of ancient **Egypt**. Ideas also came from the east through **Phoenicia**. In the 6th century BC, sculptures of the standing nude male and the standing female clothed in drapery were commonly dedicated to the gods. These sculptures stand rigidly, facing the front, with their arms at their sides. The

Greeks developed the art of sculpting the human form to a high level, and many consider that their expertise reached its height during the **Classical Age**.

Human figures were sculpted with an astonishing degree of realism but the artists were not really interested in portraying individual personalities. Instead, they tried to capture an ideal form of the human body. Even in sculptures of clothed female figures, the drapery becomes almost transparent, revealing the sculpted shape of the body beneath. It was not until the 4th century BC that sculptors began to make their figures show emotion.

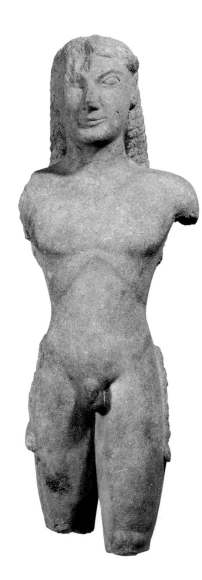

An Archaic statue of a young man. This kind of rigid figure is called a kouros.

128

Temples were decorated with sculpture. There were often friezes and panels carved in low relief on the walls, usually showing scenes from myth. A large statue of the god or goddess usually stood inside the temple. The sculptor **Phidias** was famous for the huge statues of Athena and Zeus that he made for the temples at Athens and Olympia. The triangular pediments of temples often contained sculptures carved in the round.

Above: a bronze chisel, one of the tools used by Greek sculptors. Right: instruments used by sculptors for measuring.

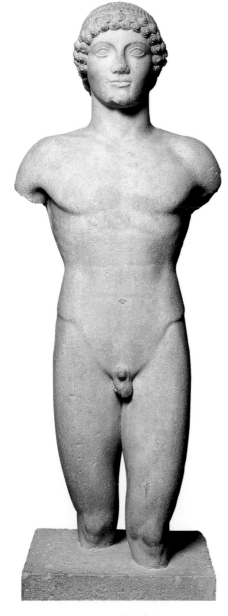

*A bronze statue of a huntsman, made in the **Hellenistic Age**.*

*A marble statue made in the **Classical Age**, about 480 BC. This famous figure is known as the Strangford Apollo.*

129

Scythians

Scythia was the name given by the ancient Greeks to an area north of the Black Sea (see map, page 5). The Scythians were a nomadic people from Iranian stock who came into contact with the Greeks as a result of trading with Greek **colonies** on the northern Black Sea coast. The Scythians were renowned for their skill as horse riders and were also famous as archers. Scythian archers were sometimes hired as **mercenaries** in Greek armies. Scythian slaves were employed to keep order in the **Assembly** in **Athens**.

Left: The Greeks seem to have been interested in their barbarian enemies, because they often featured them in art. This plate shows a non-Greek archer who may be a **Scythian**.

Below: Two ships painted on one pot. On the left is a warship, low-lying, light and speedy. Beside it is a merchant ship, high up out of the water, wide and bulky for carrying cargo.

Seafaring

The **geography** of Greece helped make **transport** by sea a central part of Greek life. However, with no compasses or other navigational instruments, seafaring could be dangerous. Sailors often played safe by keeping close to the shore and avoiding open seas. Shipwrecks seem to have been common. In the **Mediterranean** seafaring was usually confined to the summer months, when the sea was calmer.

Powerful city-states like **Athens**

depended on their **navy** in war, and sea-routes were essential for the transport of supplies of grain from the Crimea in the Black Sea. This accounts for the **colonies** that were established along the route to the Black Sea. Athenian foreign policy was governed by the need to control the sea-route from the Aegean to the narrow waterways, the Hellespont and Bosporus, which led into the Black Sea.

Shame

A sense of shame, and a keen concern with what other people might think, was a lot stronger in Greek thought than it is for most modern cultures. In the world of **Homer** the heroes place more importance on honour than on their own lives. Their sense of shame prevents them from acting in a way that would lead to the disapproval of others. Life itself was seen as a **competition** in which the dearest prize was honour and the price of failure was shame.

The idea of an individual suffering from what we call a guilty conscience was foreign to the Greeks. A sense of guilt was associated with an offence against the gods. **Croesus**, for example, was

A bronze figure of a man stabbing himself. This may be Ajax, who committed suicide out of **shame** when a prize of armour was awarded to another warrior, Odysseus, not to him.

guilty of **hubris** because he became too proud. The shedding of family blood could be a major cause of guilt, which could affect a whole community. Guilt was seen as a sort of pollution. It could only be purified with the gods' help.

Sicily

The Greeks started to colonize the large island of Sicily (see map, page 38) at the southern tip of Italy in the 8th century BC. They were attracted by its rich farmland. The most important **city-state** to be founded on Sicily was Syracuse.

Sicily did not enjoy a peaceful history. As well as fighting between different states on the island, there was a long-standing conflict between Greek settlers and Carthage. The Carthaginians were originally settlers from **Phoenicia** who founded the city of Carthage in northern Africa. They crossed the **Mediterranean** to establish colonies in parts of Sicily around the same time that Greeks began to arrive on the island.

During the **Peloponnesian War**, Athens attempted to conquer Syracuse, which was an ally of **Sparta**, but failed miserably. **Archimedes**, the great inventor, came from Syracuse.

Sieges

Laying siege to a defended city was a standard part of Greek **warfare**. However, the siege technology of the Greeks was

*Part of a stone frieze dating from the 5th century BC. It shows a city under **siege** by hoplites.*

very primitive. Often they just waited until the enemy came out to fight or was starved into surrender. Perhaps this explains why, in the story of the **Trojan War**, the siege of Troy lasted ten years.

During the **Peloponnesian War** the city of **Plataea** was besieged. The Thebans built a ramp against the city walls, hoping to gain entry over the walls, and they unsuccessfully employed a battering ram.

At the end of the 5th century BC more sophisticated siege machinery was developed in **Sicily**, including giant catapults. Further improvements in siege warfare were made by **Alexander the Great**.

Sirens

The Sirens were half-women and half-birds, who lured sailors to their death. They would sing enchanting songs to the sailors who could not resist leaving their ship to visit the Sirens' island, where they would die.

Odysseus was warned of the danger but he wanted to hear the Sirens. His crew tied him to the mast and plugged their own ears against the Sirens' songs.

*Odysseus and the **Sirens**. Odysseus is tied to the mast of his ship and his men have wax in their ears so they cannot hear the Sirens singing to them.*

Enchanted by the singing, Odysseus begged to be released but his crew followed their orders and ignored his pleadings. **Jason and the Argonauts** were also in danger of being enticed away by the Sirens, but **Orpheus** sang even more beautifully and distracted everyone's attention.

Sisyphus (Sisyphos)

In myth, Sisyphus was a clever and cunning mortal. He was punished in the Underworld (see **Hades**). He had to push a heavy stone up a hill, only for it to roll back to the bottom where he had to start all over again. His offence had been to reveal to the god of the river Asopus the whereabouts of **Zeus** and the god's daughter whom Zeus had kidnapped. Sisyphus told the god, in return for a promise of a fresh water supply for **Corinth**, a city that Sisyphus had founded.

When Zeus sent the spirit of Death, Thanatos, to claim Sisyphus, the wily mortal kidnapped Death so that for a while no one on Earth could die. Even when Sisyphus did finally die he managed to trick his way out of the Underworld. In some versions of the myth the task of rolling the stone up the hill was to keep him occupied so that he could never again escape.

Slaves

Slaves had very few rights and according to Greek law they were regarded as a form of property. If someone injured a slave, that person had to pay compensation to the slave's owner. Slaves could be bought and sold and their owners were allowed to beat them. Many slaves were owned privately but there were also public slaves. In Athens public slaves were used as security guards during meetings of the **Assembly**.

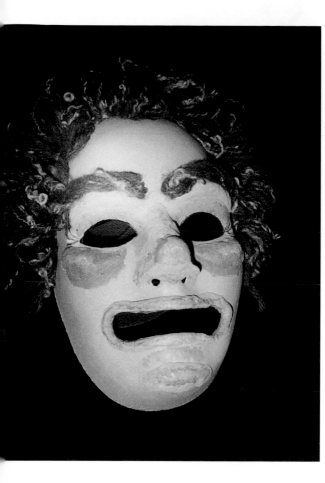

Socrates (Sokrates)

The oracle at **Delphi** proclaimed Socrates the wisest man in the world. Socrates declared that his wisdom consisted in realizing that he knew nothing at all for sure. His own motto was 'The unexamined life is not worth living.' Socrates' method of asking searching questions about the nature of truth and justice moved **philosophy** onto a new plane. In **Athens** in the 5th century BC it also led to him being branded as a dangerous thinker. He was charged with the crime of corrupting the young and of not believing in the gods of the city. He was found guilty and sentenced to death. He died in 399 BC.

Socrates is not known to have written any books himself, but his influence was so enormous that thinkers who came before him are known simply as the **Pre-Socratics**. Much of our information about Socrates is known from the works of his pupil **Plato**.

Slaves also played a part in some areas of community life. They could participate in the **Eleusinian Mysteries**, and there was a special holiday, the Kronia, when slaves could sit down and eat a meal and drink wine with their owners. Sometimes slaves were freed and given citizenship, but this did not happen often.

The number of slaves in **Athens** is estimated to have been between 80,000 and 100,000. They were mostly foreigners and made up about one-third of the city-state's population. Many slaves worked in the silver mines in Laurium, near Athens. Many were also used as private slaves in family houses. Only very poor families could not afford to have at least one slave. In law courts the evidence given by slaves was only accepted after they had been tortured. The reason for this, it seems, was the belief that unless they were tortured slaves could not be relied on to tell the truth.

A marble statue of **Socrates**.

Solon

Solon lived in **Athens** around 600 BC and played an important part in the development of **democracy**. He introduced reforms that weakened the power of the rich nobles to control the city's government. He also made ordinary farmers **citizens**, thus giving them the right to attend the **Assembly** and share political power. The laws he made were carved onto wood and preserved for public display in the **agora**. The story goes that, having made Athenians promise to obey the new laws for ten years, Solon left the city and travelled abroad. He gained a reputation for wisdom.

Sophists

The sophists were private teachers who earned their living by offering to instruct people in skills that would help them succeed in certain professions. In the **Assembly** in **Athens**, for example, people who could deliver well-argued speeches became successful politicians, and the art of speech-making was something sophists set out to teach. Rather like modern 'spin doctors' and advertisers, the sophists were criticized for being too clever and concerned not about what was right or fair, but only their ability to persuade other people.

Sophocles (Sophokles)

Sophocles was one of the great playwrights of **Athens** in the 5th century BC. He was famous in his own lifetime for his tragedies. His plays were performed at his city's annual **Dionysia** festival, where he was renowned for frequently winning the first prize. Seven of his plays have survived. One of the greatest is *Oedipus the King*, dramatizing the tragic life of **Oedipus**, and another is *Antigone*.

A bronze bust, probably Roman, of the playwright **Sophocles**. As a young man he was a performer at festivals and was noted for his dancing and singing.

Sparta

Sparta was one of the strongest **city-states** in ancient Greece. Sparta and **Athens** are the two city-states about which most is known, but they were very different in character. Sparta was never a democracy. It was ruled by two kings at a time. Sparta played an important part in helping Greece win the **Persian Wars**. After this, relations with Athens did not go well. Sparta felt threatened by the development of the **Athenian Empire** and by Athenian **democracy**. This led to the **Peloponnesian War**.

After defeating Athens, Sparta reached the height of its power. A treaty was made with Persia around 386 BC, known as the King's Peace. Sparta

The site of the once mighty city of **Sparta**.

*This bronze figurine of a **Spartan** warrior shows the traditional image of a Spartan: a grim and fearsome fighter.*

allowed Persia to regain control over the Greek states of **Ionia**, but was finally defeated by **Thebes** in 371 BC, after which Sparta never regained its former power.

Sparta's Legacy

The word 'spartan' has entered the English language as an adjective describing endurance of harsh conditions. The first of the eight towns called 'Sparta' in the United States was so named in 1852 because the pioneers felt they shared some of the Spartan qualities of courage and perseverance.

Spartans

Fear of rebellion by the **helots** encouraged Sparta to develop into an intensely military state. The helots were a people whom Sparta had conquered and then enslaved.

The soldiers of most other city-states earned their living mostly as farmers when they were not called on to fight. By contrast, Spartan men were trained from a young age to become part of a full-time professional army. From the age of seven, boys left their families and were brought up very strictly by the state to become

Stadium (Stadion)

The ancient Greek word *stadion* referred to a flat piece of ground where athletic events took place during **festivals** or sports competitions like the **Olympic Games**. Sometimes a nearby slope provided a convenient place for spectators to sit. All ancient Greek stadia were about 200 metres (600 feet) in length. Sometimes, as at the **Delphi** stadium, one end of the stadium was rounded, but the track did not curve round the inside of the stadium like a modern running track. All ancient races were run in a straight line. The track was made of clay, covered with sand.

Turning posts were fixed in the ground near the ends of the stadium, so that runners had space in which to

soldiers. Boys were not fed very well and if they were caught stealing they were punished, not for stealing but for being caught. There is a story of a Spartan boy who stole a young fox and hid it under his cloak. The animal gnawed into his body, but the boy died rather than cry out and make his theft known.

Young Spartans were encouraged to fight one another, but never in anger, and cowardice was like a crime. A Spartan mother is said to have remarked to her son as he left for war, 'Come back with your shield – or on it.' In other words, it was better to die and be carried home on your shield than endure the **shame** of losing it. Even when a Spartan married he remained living in military barracks until the age of thirty and was expected to visit his wife in secret.

Spartan **women** had lives very different from most women in ancient Greece. They received an **education** and, because Spartan **men** were often away from home, they had more control over affairs than most Greek women did.

*This model is a reconstruction of the **stadium** at Olympia where the original **Olympic Games** took place. Athletes raced along a straight track. Spectators sat on the sloping side of the hill of Kronos. Competitors entered the stadium through a tunnel, part of which still remains at Olympia.*

turn around. The blowing of a trumpet would signal the start of a race. Stone sills on the ground, with grooves for the runners' toes, marked the start line. There were no starting blocks. Athletes began their races from a standing position.

Symposium

A symposium was a drinking party attended by rich men after an evening meal. Snacks were served on a low table and **slaves** poured **wine** while the male guests reclined on couches conversing and enjoying each other's company. Sometimes women were hired to provide entertainment. Occasionally the men amused themselves by playing a game called *kottabos*, which involved flicking drops of wine left behind in a drinking cup at a target.

*Below: a young man and a slave girl at a **symposium**.*

*Above: the **stadium** at Delphi as it is today.*

The word 'tantalize' (or 'tantalise') comes from the myth of Tantalus. It means to torment or tease by the promise of something that is not obtainable.

Tantalus (Tantalos)

Tantalus was a king, famous for the punishment he had to endure in the Underworld (see **Hades**). He stood in water up to his neck, but whenever he tried to take a drink, the water evaporated before his eyes. At the same time, a branch laden with tasty fruit hung just above his head. Whenever he tried to reach some fruit, the branch would move back, teasingly out of reach.

There are different accounts of the crime for which Tantalus was being punished. In one story, he set out to test the knowledge of the gods by inviting them to a feast where he served them with the flesh of his own son whom he had murdered. Only **Demeter** ate some of the flesh, because her mind was distracted at the time by the loss of her daughter Persephone. The other gods realized what he had done.

Temples

Temples were the houses of the gods. During festivals and on other special occasions, people would gather at the altar to perform **sacrifices** in honour of the god. The altar was always outside the

*The entrance to a Classical Greek **temple**. There are two rows of Doric columns (see **architecture**). The building is decorated with elaborate marble sculpture.*

A model of the **Temple** of Zeus at Olympia.

main building: ordinary people were not allowed to enter the temple. A statue of the god stood inside the temple, tended by **priests and priestesses**.

Important temples became wealthy from gifts made to the gods. Sometimes a temple would function like a bank, storing and occasionally lending money.

The first temples were made of mud-bricks and wood. Later, stone was used for the walls and columns of temples (see **architecture**). Wooden beams supported a roof of clay or marble tiles.

Thales

Thales was the first 'scientist' and philosopher of whom anything is known, though none of his writings have survived. He lived in **Ionia** (see map, page 23) sometime around 600 BC. Legend records that he predicted a solar eclipse. If so, his prediction was probably based upon astronomical data gathered by the Egyptians or the Babylonians. Thales did travel to **Egypt**, but whether knowledge at the time was sufficient to predict an eclipse is uncertain. Thales taught that everything had its origin in water. This theory too may have come from Egypt. In Egyptian **creation myths** a watery state existed before the world began.

Theatres

Theatres in ancient Greece were open to the sky. They were built out of the side of a hill, and the ground at the foot of the hill was levelled out for the stage area. The stage may have been slightly raised, but not as high as in a modern theatre. In front of the stage was the *orchestra*, where the chorus danced and sang (a plan of a theatre is shown on the next page).

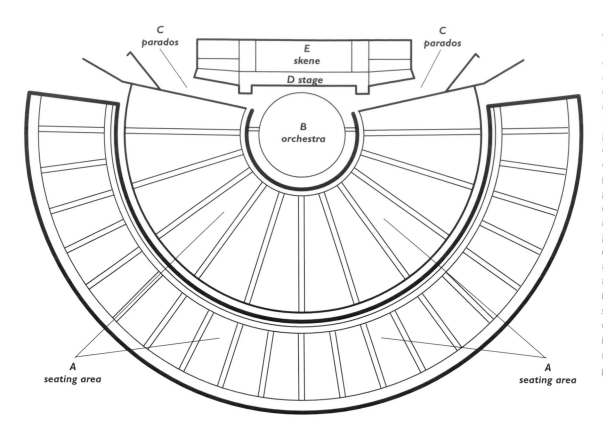

C
parados

C
parados

E
skene

D stage

B
orchestra

A
seating area

A
seating area

A plan of a Greek **theatre**. The seating areas (**A**), which could hold 15,000 people or more, sloped down to a large circular area of flattened earth known as the orchestra (**B**). This was where the chorus of performers would sing and dance. They entered and left by a passageway known as the parados (**C**). The actors performed in a special stage area (**D**) behind the orchestra. Behind the stage was an area for a stage-building (**E**) made of wood. The Greek name for this was skene, which gives us the word 'scenery'. The Greeks, however, did not have elaborate scenery. The back wall, which was about 4.5 metres (15 feet) high, would simply be painted to represent the front of a palace and a couple of doors.

Most of the Greek plays that are known today were written and first performed in the 5th century BC. Stone **theatres** were only built later. Many theatres were remodelled by the Romans, but this one at Epidaurus (below) still preserves its original form.

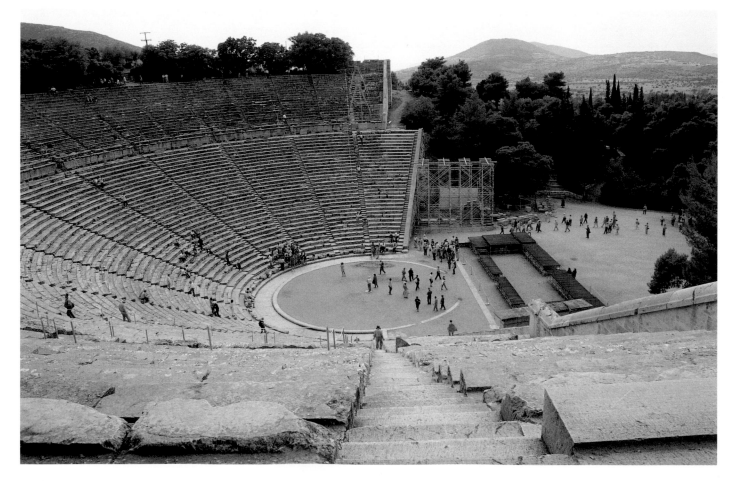

Thebes

The city of Thebes (see map, page 62) was one of the strongest in the Greek world. It was important in myth and in the early history of Greece. Thebes dominated the central region of ancient Greece called Boeotia, and was renowned for its army. Thebans were famous for their long lances and their use of **cavalry** in **warfare**.

Thebes was powerful in **Mycenaean** times, and later became an **oligarchy**. For centuries, Thebes was in conflict with **Athens**, which lay some 60 kilometres (40 miles) to the southeast. When **Persia** invaded Greece in 480 BC, Thebes was the only major Greek power to ally itself with **Xerxes**. After the defeat of the Persians, the reputation of Thebes was badly affected. Its influence was only revived by **Sparta**, who wanted an ally against Athens in the **Peloponnesian War**.

After the war, Thebes fell out with Sparta and made an alliance with its old enemy, Athens. Then, with the aid of **Corinth** and Argos, Thebes waged war against Sparta in the Corinthian War (394–386 BC). The mighty Spartan army was defeated at the Battle of Leuctra in 371 BC. The Thebans, led by an elite group of 300 hoplites called the 'Sacred Band', marched into the Peloponnese and freed the **helots** of Messenia.

Some thirty years later, Thebes was defeated by **Macedon**. After the Thebans had staged an unsuccessful rebellion in 335 BC, **Alexander the Great** wiped out the city of Thebes. Those who were not killed were sold into slavery. Thebes was later rebuilt but never recovered its power. Today the ancient city lies buried under the modern town.

Thermopylae

Thermopylae was a narrow pass between the mountains and the sea in central Greece. There, in 480 BC, a small Greek army held back the invading **Persians** for three days. A Greek traitor, named Ephialtes, told the Persians about a

The site of the Battle of **Thermopylae**, *where some 5,000 Greeks under the command of King Leonidas of Sparta held back a huge Persian army of as many as 200,000 men.*

footpath that would bring them down behind the Greeks. The Greeks suddenly found themselves hemmed in from both sides. They fought to the last hoplite. It was a huge military defeat for the Greeks, but it was seen as a moral and emotional victory. A famous epitaph at the pass commemorates the Spartan dead:

Go tell the Spartans, stranger passing by,
That here, obedient to their word, we lie.

Theseus

Theseus was a mythical hero of Athens. His most famous exploit was to kill the Minotaur. King **Minos** of **Crete** had been forcing **Athens** to send him seven young men and women every year. He fed them to the Minotaur, a monster who lived in a maze beneath his palace.

Theseus was aided by **Ariadne**, King Minos' daughter. She fell in love with Theseus and showed him how to find his way in and out of the Minotaur's maze using a ball of thread. Theseus killed the monster with her help, but then he abandoned her. He returned to Athens where he became king. He went to fight the **Amazons**, returning with Hippolyta, the Amazon queen. She died after bearing him a son, Hippolytus. Then Theseus married Ariadne's sister Phaedra, but this marriage also ended in tragedy when she fell in love with Hippolytus.

Theseus and the Minotaur, a monster who was part-man, part-bull.

Theseus does battle with the Minotaur, after **Ariadne** has shown him the way through the maze where it lives.

Thesmophoria

The Thesmophoria was a **festival** held throughout Greece. Unusually for a Greek festival, it was attended by **women** only. The festival was associated with the worship of **Demeter**, the goddess of agriculture. It was a fertility ritual designed to ensure the success of planted crops.

In Athens the festival lasted three days. All the women left their homes and met together on the Pnyx. (Normally **Assembly** meetings took place on the Pnyx and women were not allowed to attend.) The second day of the festival was spent fasting, but on the final day the women feasted and had a party.

Above: a Thessalian coin. Horsemen from **Thessaly** *were famous and contributed greatly to the victories of* **Alexander the Great**.

deposits of gold and silver and because it could supply grain, timber and **slaves**.

Characters from Greek **myth**, including **Orpheus** and **Eurydice**, were associated with Thrace.

Thrace consisted of what is now north-east Greece, western Turkey, and part of Bulgaria.

Thucydides (Thoukydides)

Thucydides was an historian from **Athens** who lived in the 5th century BC. He wrote an account of the **Peloponnesian War** as it was happening. Unlike the Greek historian **Herodotus**, who came before him, Thucydides did not bring **myth** and fables into his writing, and his work reads more like that of a modern historian.

Thucydides served as a general in the Athenian army. He described his own failure to prevent **Sparta** from capturing an Athenian colony in **Thrace**. On account of this failure, he was banished for a number of years by the Athenians.

Thessaly

Thessaly (see map, page 62) is an area of north-eastern Greece made up of two large plains surrounded by mountains. Thessaly features in many myths and legends. It was usually described as a wild and lawless place: the home of **Pan**, witches and **Centaurs**, the land where **Jason** was born and where Mount **Olympus** towered over the landscape. Thessaly's broad plains made it suitable for raising horses, and Thessalian armies – unlike most Greek forces – consisted mainly of **cavalry**.

Thrace

Below: a Thracian coin. The Greeks saw fighters from **Thrace** *as savage warriors.*

Thrace (see map, page 62) was a region to the north-east of Greece, outside the main Greek world. However, it attracted Greek **colonies** because of its rich

Toys and games

Hoops, spinning tops, yo-yos, rattles, rocking horses, swings, seesaws, dolls, dolls' houses and models of horses and carts were all favourite toys and games of ancient Greek children. Children also played a version of 'heads or tails', using pieces of broken pottery – potsherds – and dividing into two teams. Depending on which side of the potsherd landed on the ground, one team would chase members of the other team and try to catch them. They also played a game resembling blind-man's buff. The game of jacks, or knucklebones, was popular with adults as well as children. Another game involved trying to hit a stone target by throwing things at it. If your throw landed farthest from the target, you had to try and reach the target blindfolded while giving a piggyback ride to another player.

Children also kept pets. Dogs and tame hares were the favourites. Cats and rabbits were uncommon, and hardly known to the Greeks. When a girl was ready to be married, the young bride would renounce her toys and dedicate them to the gods. Cockfighting was a popular pastime for those who could afford leisure time, and would be watched by older children.

Transport

The **geography of Greece** influenced Greek methods of transport. Ships (see **seafaring**) were the commonest means of long-distance travel. On land, people travelled by foot or on horseback, and used mules to transport heavy loads. The Greeks did not develop an organized system of roads, as the Romans did (see **Rome**), but there were some paved

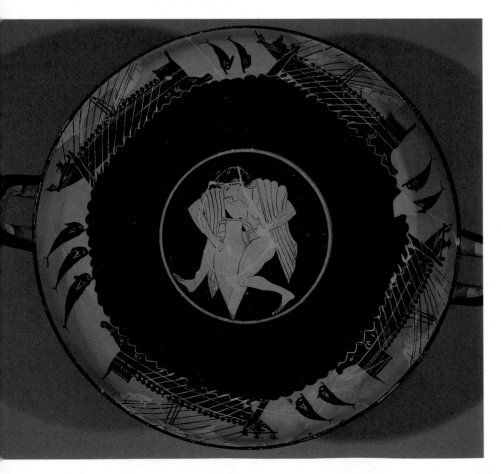

*Above: clay figures of animals, like this pig, were popular children's **toys** in ancient Greece.*

*Below: cargo ships sail round the rim of this cup. In the centre a man moves an amphora, a large pot used for the **transport** of oil, wine and other goods.*

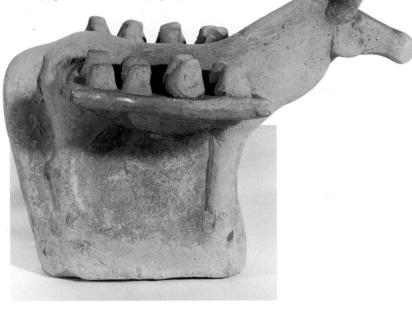

*Mules were used for the **transport** of goods overland. This small clay figure shows a mule carrying trays of cheeses.*

roads. On the whole, wheeled vehicles were not common. There were chariots, drawn by horses and mainly used in racing. Mules were used to pull two-wheeled carts and four-wheeled wagons.

Large merchant ships, too big to be rowed by oars, sailed the seas when a favourable wind was behind them. Journeys by sea took a long time when a ship had to zigzag its way through an unfavourable wind. Ships kept close to

the land whenever they could. Greek sailors navigated using landmarks and the sun. Unlike warships (see **warfare**), merchant transport ships often used **slaves** as crew.

Trojan War

In myth, the Trojan War began when the Trojan prince **Paris** ran off with the Greek **Helen**. The Greeks sailed to the city of **Troy** and laid **siege** to it for ten years before finally achieving victory. The story of this epic struggle was immortalized by the poet **Homer** in the **Iliad**.

The poem tells of the deeds of many of the heroes who took part in the war. They include the Greeks **Achilles**, **Ajax**, **Agamemnon** and **Odysseus** and the Trojans **Hector** and **Paris**. The Trojan War heaped honour and glory on some but it also brought death and tragedy – not only to warriors but also to women like **Cassandra** and **Iphigenia**. The end of the war came about when the Greeks used the **Wooden Horse** to trick their way into the city. The Greeks then destroyed the city, killed all the Trojan men and sold the women and children into slavery.

*The **Trojan War** ended cruelly for many of the Trojans. Here, the Greeks sacrifice Polyxena, the daughter of the Trojan king and queen, to appease the ghost of **Achilles**. It is unusual for scenes of sacrifice on Greek pots to be so gory.*

*The **siege** of **Troy** ends bloodily. The Greek warrior Neoptolemus hurls the baby son of **Hector** onto the body of King Priam lying on the altar. He will kill them both. Some legends tell how Neoptolemus was prevented from reaching home after the **Trojan War** as a punishment from the gods for killing Priam like this.*

Troy

Troy is best known from the epic tale related by **Homer** in the **Iliad**. Before the opening of that story, the Trojan prince **Paris** had brought **Helen** to Troy from Greece, so causing the **Trojan War**. The city of Troy was across the Aegean Sea from Greece, on the northwest coast of **Asia Minor** (see map, page 62).

The site of Troy was found by the 19th-century archaeologist Heinrich Schliemann. In 1870 Schliemann discovered at Hissarlik in Turkey the site of the real city of Troy. His excavations showed that there had been walled settlements on the site long before the rise of Greece. Schliemann found that, sometime around 1220 BC, a great fire had destroyed what archaeologists call Troy VIIa. It is very tempting to believe – and it is quite possible – that this burning of the city is the destruction of Troy that Homer describes.

The location of Troy, close to the Hellespont and the route to the Black Sea, may explain why a city developed and prospered there. It might also explain why the Mycenaean Greeks (see **Mycenaean civilization**) would have gone to war against Troy. That part of Asia Minor was a valuable trading region and whoever controlled the Hellespont was in a powerful position to dominate the trade route.

Tyranny

Many Greek **city-states**, especially in the 6th century BC, were ruled by one supremely powerful dictator, called a tyrant. Such men took power by force. Tyrants were usually of noble birth but they often had the support of the poorer classes. The rule of a tyrant was like the rule of a king, but of course tyrants did not inherit royal power. Pisistratos made himself tyrant of **Athens** in 546 BC, and his rule was beneficial to the city.

War

War was very common in ancient Greece. During the **Classical Age** the **city-state** of **Athens** was at peace, on average, less than one year in every three. The history of another powerful city-state, **Thebes**, reads like one long list of wars against other states. Wars were common and, according to the philosopher **Heraclitus**, 'War is the father of all things.'

We know a lot about war, compared to some other aspects of Greek civilization. This is because historians like **Herodotus**, **Thucydides** and **Xenophon** wrote about war, and wars featured prominently in Greek literature and **myth**.

War was seen as a natural part of life in ancient Greece. It was elevated to a high level of honour and esteem, but it was not glorified. The Greeks did not deny or ignore the terrible sense of loss caused by death, or the brutality and violence of war. They accepted these things, but they had a strong sense that it was worth the suffering. However, the Greeks did not attribute any special qualities to Ares, their god of war.

Warfare

Warfare in the time of the **Mycenaean civilization** seems to have centred on duels between heroic noblemen. This, at

Greeks at **war**. Two helmeted Greek warriors confront one another on this plate. One of them will suffer the same fate as the man lying at their feet.

'No one is so foolish as to prefer war to peace: in peace children bury their fathers, while in war fathers bury their children.'

Herodotus

least, was the picture presented by the poet **Homer** in his descriptions of warriors like **Achilles** and **Ajax**. The warriors first threw spears at each other and then fought with their swords, using shields for protection and chariots for battle transport.

In the **Classical Age**, warfare had less to do with individuals and more to do with armies of **citizens**. On land, warfare was usually conducted by rival teams of foot soldiers – hoplites – fighting in close formations on an open plain. Soldiers stood together, shields overlapping, while pushing and thrusting with their swords and spears (see **armour and arms**) against the enemy. The critical moment in a battle came when one side's formation of hoplites buckled and began to break up under the superior force and stamina of the other side.

Farming methods and the mountainous **geography of Greece** did not encourage the keeping of horses, and **cavalry** was not the main part of an army. The shortage of good farming land meant that battles were often fought for possession of the fertile plains. On flat ground, set-piece close-formation battles were possible, and archers or lightly armed soldiers were of less importance than the heavily clad hoplites.

Naval battles, such as **Salamis**, involved the use of triremes. These were fighting ships crewed by up to 200 oarsmen. The rowers sat in three banks, one above the other, on either side of the vessel. Steering oars were at the stern of the trireme, and a bronze-plated pointed ram extended from the prow. The single mast and sail were removed before rowing into battle. The ships had to stay close to land, as there was no room for supplies on board.

The power of **Athens** depended very much on its fleet of 200 triremes. This meant that there were about 35,000 rowers. They could exert political pressure on the **city-state** because they were vital to its security. Since most of the rowers were among the less wealthy Athenian citizens, their importance increased the political power of the poorer people in the **democracy**.

Washing and cosmetics

It is known that the Greeks took baths, but how regularly they washed is not known. There was no soap. Instead they cleaned themselves by rubbing olive oil onto the skin and then scraping it off with a tool called a *strigil*.

A bronze figurine of an Etruscan youth. He is cleaning his body with a strigil.

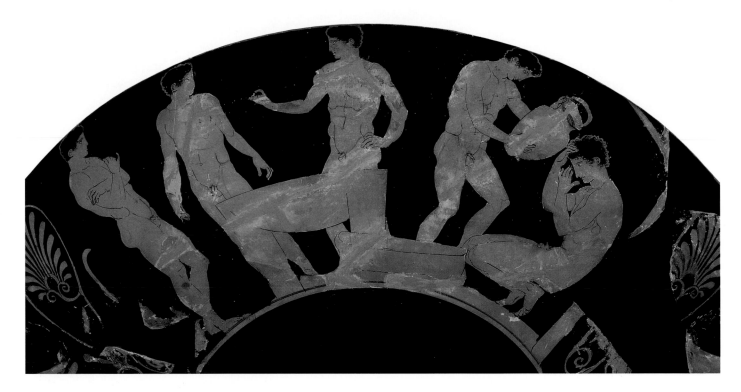

*This illustration from a drinking cup shows one athlete helping another by **washing** the dust out of his hair. Beside them, another athlete uses a strigil to remove the dust from his skin.*

*This illustration from a drinking cup shows one athlete helping another by **washing** the dust out of his hair. Beside them, another athlete uses a strigil to remove the dust from his skin.*

***Washing** equipment: a brass pot for olive oil and a set of strigils.*

Archaeologists have uncovered evidence of mirrors, which were made from polished bronze, as well as razors and even manicure sets. People used toothpicks and whitening powders to keep their teeth clean, and special remedies were available for the problem of bad breath.

Perfume was made by adding scented flowers and spices to oil. Women used certain plants and types of seaweed as a form of rouge. They highlighted their eyebrows and eyelids using charcoal. Women also liked to lighten the colour of their skin, which they did by applying a specially prepared whitener made from lead and vinegar.

Different kinds of pots (see **pottery**) were specially made for washing purposes and for cosmetics.

Water

Water was essential not just for drinking but also for **washing**, laundry and cooking. From the **Classical Age** onwards there were public baths, and some wealthy people's houses had their own bathroom.

Water was drawn from wells, and underground cisterns were built to store rainwater. Well-covers were made of stone or pottery. Sometimes a pulley system was attached to the well-head, to ease the task of drawing up water from a pot tied to the end of a rope.

There were also public fountains where the water, flowing from a spring or aqueduct, was fed through metal spouts. **Archaeology** has uncovered clay piping, but this may have been used more for drainage than for the supply of water.

The importance of water to the ancient Greeks is shown by the fact that springs were often seen as places sacred to the gods. Water also played a symbolic role in some religious rituals. Before a **sacrifice** there was a ritual washing of the hands and a special kind of metal pot was used for holding the water.

*A vase painting showing women collecting **water** from a public fountain. There are stone blocks for the heavy water jugs to rest on.*

Wine

Wine was the commonest drink of the ancient Greeks. It was nearly always heavily diluted with **water**. Most Greeks disapproved of anybody who drank strong wine undiluted. The production and export of wine went on throughout the Greek world. Harvesting grapes was an important part of the **farming** calendar. After the grape juice fermented, it was stored in clay amphoras (see **pottery**). Another type of pot, the *krater*, was used for mixing water with the wine before drinking.

Sometimes perfumes were added to give the wine a special flavour and increase its value. Honey, too, might be added to wine, as the Greeks liked sweet drinks.

Women

From what is known about life in **Athens** it is clear that women were treated as second-class citizens. They could not attend the **Assembly** to vote, they could not be jurors in the **law courts** or become public officials and they could not inherit property. The only way a written will was allowed in Athens was when there was no son to inherit the family property. It often happened that a woman who was an only child had to marry her father's brother to keep the estate in the family. Like women, **men** who were **slaves**, and men who lived in the city but were not **citizens,** were also denied many rights.

Women from wealthier families had little opportunity to mix socially with anyone outside of their family. At home, they had their own quarters and were not

*The paintings on these white-ground pots show **women** in domestic scenes: one is dressing, and another is looking at her jewellery.*

*A Greek family shown on a marble gravestone, called a stela, made in the **Hellenistic Age**.*
*It shows a woman called Metreis standing beside her husband, Exakestes. Metreis is holding a spindle, a symbol of the role of **women** in the home. She and her husband are clasping hands in an affectionate gesture - perhaps saying goodbye. The small figures on either side may be servants or they may be the couple's children.*

usually seen in public. Women in poorer families, who did not have slaves to do everyday jobs such as fetching **water** and washing **clothes**, had more opportunities to mix with other women.

There were some ritual occasions when women played a major role. For example, the festival of **Thesmophoria** was one in which only citizen women could participate. Women also played an important part in some other festivals (see **Eleusinian Mysteries**) and at **funerals**.

After **marriage** a woman's duty was to bear children and bring them up, look after the family slaves and run the household. Because of the big difference in the age at which men and women got married, many women became widows in their early thirties.

Wooden Horse

In myth, the **Trojan War** dragged on for ten years before the wily Greek hero **Odysseus** devised a plan to trick the Trojans and capture their city.

Odysseus persuaded his fellow-Greeks to build a huge wooden horse, big enough to hide a small force of soldiers inside. The Greeks left the horse outside the walls of Troy, then pretended to sail away, back to Greece. Secretly they anchored their ships just off the coast once they were out of sight.

The Trojans, thinking the horse was a farewell offering to the gods, brought it inside their city and celebrated the end of the war. The Greek army crept back to Troy under cover of darkness. During the night, the Greeks inside the horse climbed out and opened the city gates for their army. The Greeks poured inside, and the war was won.

*This modern reconstruction of the **Wooden Horse** greets visitors to the site of ancient **Troy**, at Hissarlik, near the west coast of Turkey.*

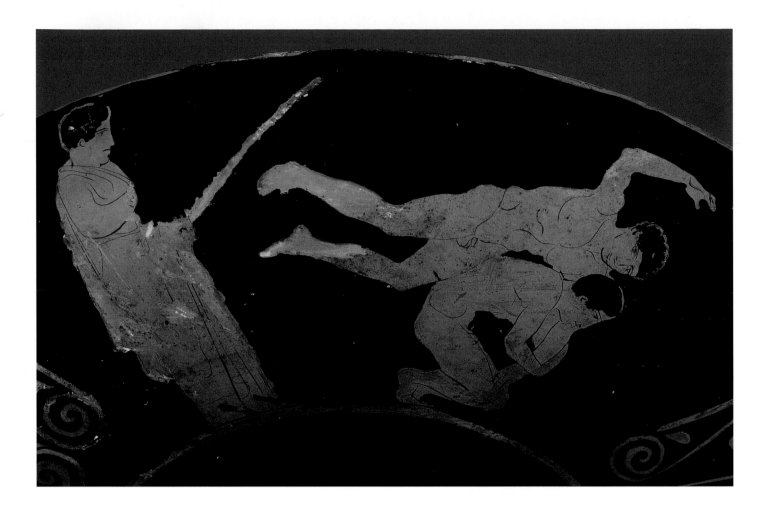

Wrestling

Wrestling is a very ancient sport. It probably came to ancient Greece from the east and it may have been known as early as the **Mycenaean civilization**. Wrestling bouts are mentioned by **Homer** and one of the many legends about the hero **Heracles** concerns his wrestling match with a giant called Antaeus. Antaeus lived in North **Africa**. He forced everyone he met to wrestle with him and when he beat them, he would kill them. Heracles, however, defeated the giant and killed him.

Most Greek towns had an area set aside for wrestling. It was called the *palaestra*. The sport of wrestling was a part of every boy's **education**. Wrestling bouts were included in the major competitions in **athletics**. There were rules in

*A **wrestling** bout. One wrestler throws his opponent over his shoulder while a judge, or perhaps a trainer, looks on.*

wrestling, but unlike the modern sport there were no weight divisions.

Each wrestler tried to achieve a 'fall' against his opponent. That meant either holding down the opponent so that his back and shoulders, or his chest and stomach, stayed on the ground; or pinning the opponent in a hold from which he could not release himself. The winner of a wrestling bout during an athletics competition was the first wrestler to gain three falls.

Writing and reading

The earliest-known form of Greek writing dates from the **Mycenaean civilization**. It was found on tablets of clay and is called Linear B. This writing died out with the collapse of Mycenaean culture. Sometime in the early 8th century BC, the Greek alphabet was developed from Phoenician writing. The modern Greek alphabet is the same as the one used to write down the works of **Homer**, around 750 BC, and the works of literature and philosophy in the **Classical Age**.

Originally, the Greeks started a line of writing at the right end and worked across to the left. Then, if a second line was required, the writing moved from the left back to the right end. The Greek name for this method of writing means 'ox-turning', because that was how the Greeks ploughed their fields. By the 5th century BC, writing moved only from left to right. There were only 'capital' letters, written separately, and there was little or no space left between words. There was very little punctuation. TOUSTHISSEEMSAVERYDIFFICULTWAYO FWRITINGANDREADINGBUTITWASQUITE NORMALFORGREEKS.

During the **Classical Age** people in Greece usually wrote on papyrus, made from the pith of the papyrus plant. The papyrus came from **Egypt**, the only place where it grew. Strips of papyrus were pressed together into sheets, which were then glued together to form one long roll, because papyrus does not fold easily. The roll, sometimes up to 9 metres (30 feet) in length, was fastened at both ends with wooden rollers to form a scroll. Such scrolls were the earliest 'books'. They could be unrolled bit by bit in the course of reading, like turning pages.

Inscriptions for the general public to read were carved on stone tablets or

Greek writing materials and equipment. On the left is a wax tablet (delton) and a sheet of papyrus is on the right. In front you can see an ink-holder, two pens and two styli.

painted wooden panels and displayed in public places. The ancient Greeks always read aloud and never silently to themselves.

For writing on papyrus they used a thin reed pen and ink that was made of a mixture of a vegetable gum and carbon. Shorter notes and letters could be written on hollowed-out wooden tablets covered with wax. The writer used a stylus to mark letters into the wax. The tablets could be reused by melting and replacing the wax.

R eading the label

The title of the piece of writing on a roll of papyrus usually appeared at the very end. This was because the final sheet was protected by the roller, whereas the beginning of the roll was more likely to suffer wear and tear. The contents of a roll could also be identified by a label (sillybos) on the outside.

X

Xenophon

Xenophon was a writer and mercenary soldier from **Athens**. In 401 BC he joined an expedition of 10,000 Greek **mercenaries** hired by a Persian prince to help him take over the kingdom of **Persia**. The Greeks landed at Sardis, marched deep into Persian territory and won an important battle at Cunaxa. However, the Persian prince who was paying them was killed in the battle, so they decided to set off home.

Xenophon wrote an account of his adventures during this expedition. His book, *Anabasis* (*March Up-Country*), was the first lengthy autobiography to be written down. It tells the exciting story of how five out of six Greeks made their way through unknown territory back to the Black Sea, after a series of dangerous adventures that lasted three years from the time they first left Sardis.

The map below shows the course of this famous March of the Ten Thousand.

*The map shows the astonishing journey undertaken by **Xenophon** and his mercenaries.*

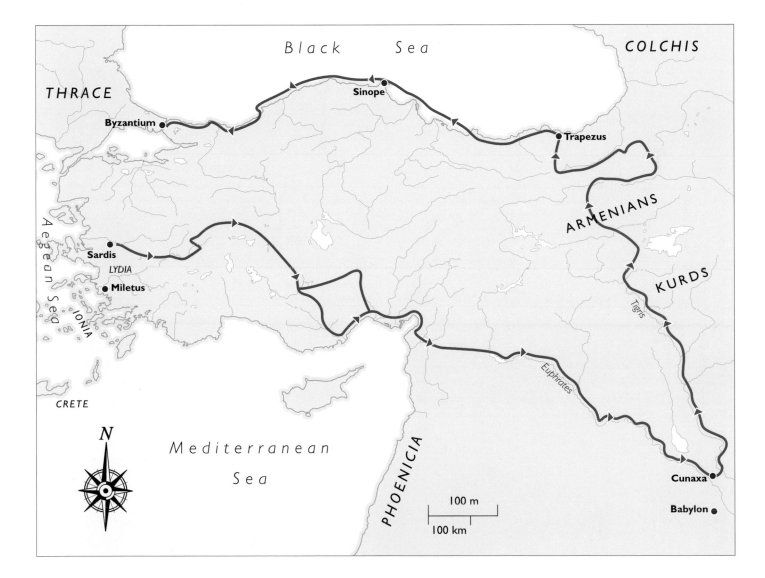

Xerxes

Xerxes was king of Persia from 486 to 465 BC. He planned and led an invasion of Greece in 480 BC. At first, Xerxes achieved success by defeating the Greeks at **Thermopylae** and he was able to march unopposed into **Athens**. This gave him the confidence to attack the Greek fleet at **Salamis**, but he was defeated. He left his army in Greece under the command of one of his generals while he returned to Persia.

The historian **Herodotus** portrays Xerxes as a man capable of philosophical reflection. He described how Xerxes wept as he watched his vast army march across the Hellespont from Asia to Europe because he realized that in a hundred years' time all of them would be dead. But, to Herodotus, Xerxes was also guilty of **hubris**. He paid for his pride by having his mighty empire humbled by the Greeks.

*The map shows the route taken by the navy (in red) and land army (in green) of **Xerxes** from his bases in Asia Minor.*

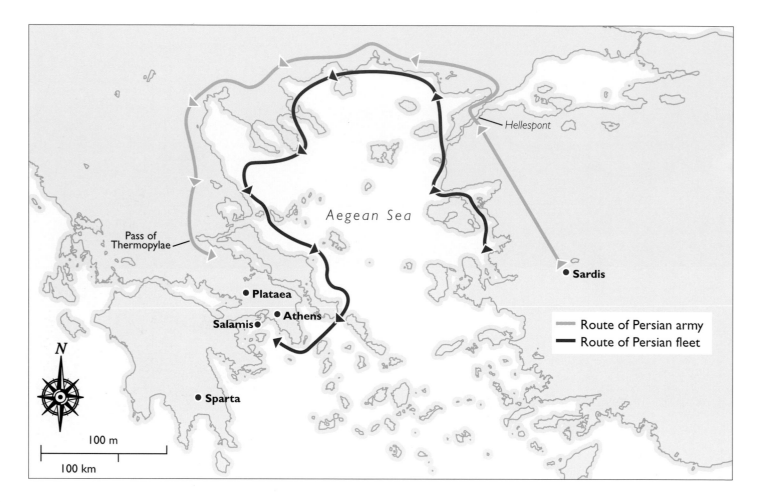

Hellespont

Aegean Sea

Pass of Thermopylae

Sardis

Plataea

Athens

Salamis

Sparta

N

100 m

100 km

—— Route of Persian army
—— Route of Persian fleet

Z

Zeus

Zeus was the chief of the Greek gods, the controller of thunder and lightning and the dispenser of justice. He was the most powerful of all the gods on Mount **Olympus**, and he was subject only to the dictates of **fate**.

Zeus came to power after he overthrew the Titans (see **creation myth**). He and his two brothers, the gods **Hades** and **Poseidon**, divided up the world amongst themselves.

Zeus was married to his sister, the goddess **Hera**, but he had many love affairs with other goddesses and mortal women. He was the father of **Athena**, **Apollo**, **Artemis**, **Hermes** and **Dionysus**. Leaving Olympus, Zeus came down to earth and became the father of **Helen** of Troy and of many other children, including the hero **Heracles**.

Competitions in **athletics** were held in honour of Zeus at Olympia. A temple built there housed a giant statue of the god, which was one of the Seven Wonders of the Ancient World. The statue of Zeus at Olympia was made by the famous sculptor **Phidias**.

The ancient Greek city of Elis used a portrait of Zeus on its silver coins.

Index